Your First Interview

Everything You Need To Know To "Ace" The Interview Process And Get Your First Job

Other Books by Ron Fry:

Your First Resume
How To Study

Your First Interview

Everything You Need To Know To "Ace" The Interview Process And Get Your First Job

By Ron Fry

THE CAREER PRESS
62 BEVERLY RD.,
PO BOX 34
HAWTHORNE, NJ 07507
1-800-CAREER-1
201-427-0229 (OUTSIDE U.S.)
FAX: 201-427-2037

Copyright © 1991 by Ron Fry

YOUR FIRST INTERVIEW: Everything You Need to Know to "Ace" the Interview Process and Get Your First Job
ISBN 0-934829-67-5, $8.95

A number of examples from the author's life and career are cited. All names of actual people have been changed and, in many cases, two or more person's experiences combined into a single example. All names and addresses cited in various letters are fictitious. Any similarities between names, addresses, experiences or jobs used as examples with any persons living or dead are purely coincidental.

Copies of this volume may be ordered by mail or phone directly from the publisher. To order by mail, please include price as noted above, $2.50 handling per order, plus $1.00 for each book ordered. Send to: The Career Press Inc., 62 Beverly Rd., PO Box 34, Hawthorne, NJ 07507

Or call Toll-Free 1-800-CAREER-1 (in Canada: 201-427-0229) to order using your VISA or Mastercard or for further information on all books published or distributed by The Career Press.

Table of Contents

Your First Interview

Introduction
Welcome To The Real World   7
Trust me. This isn't college anymore

Chapter 1
Getting to Know Them   11
The importance of company research

Chapter 2
Getting the Interview   21
Homework really does pay off

Chapter 3
Developing a Personal Inventory   33
Just who do you think you are?

Chapter 4
Not The Spanish Inquisition!   55
What to expect during your first interview

Chapter 5

Here There Be Dragons   69

The interview with the hiring manager

Chapter 6

Walk Right In, Sit Right Down   83

You don't get a second chance
at first impressions

Chapter 7

In The Spotlight   91

The finer points of interviewee technique

Chapter 8

And The Survey Says   103

66 favorite interview questions of all time

Chapter 9

Are You Buying?   115

The interview is a two-way street

Chapter 10

What Did You Say?   123

Your rights as an interviewee

Chapter 11

Bet You're Glad That's Over   131

But it isn't—until you follow up

Chapter 12

Back In The Classroom Again   137

Did you learn anything from the interview?

Chapter 13

Negotiating Your First Salary   143

You want to be _paid_ for working here?

Index   151

Introduction

Welcome To The Real World

Trust Me. This Isn't College Anymore

Those already working at a company can always spot the candidates waiting for their first interviews.

There they are in the reception area, rows of impeccably dressed collegiates in standard-issue blue interview suits.

Their heartbeats are almost audible.

They all seem afflicted with Macbeth Syndrome, constantly rubbing their palms on their thighs in hopes of drying them before they have to shake the interviewer's hand.

Their hair is perfect, though unmessable by anything short of a direct ICBM strike.

Will you be any different? Probably not.

If you are alive, you will almost surely be nervous before, during and after your first job interview. The prospect of convincing a total stranger to invest his or her company's money and time in you probably *should* produce some anxiety.

But you will be even *more* nervous if you are *unable* to clearly articulate your goals and ambitions, *unconfident* in your skills and abilities, and *unprepared* to discuss them.

What the 1990s Have
In Store For You

But wait a minute, you say. Sure, I'll be a little nervous for the interview, but the 1990s are going to be a sellers' market, so getting a job will be no sweat.

Well, in some ways that's true, but the 1990s will also see companies become more selective than ever before. They'll simply have to be. The high cost of training new employees, the legal difficulties frequently presented when employers fire people who don't work out, and the increase in global competitiveness have made the selection process more rigorous than ever.

Corporate America is spending more money than ever before on psychological tests, honesty tests, drug tests, assessments, and computerized screening systems.

They are sending recruiters and supervisors to courses on interviewing and candidate evaluation procedures.

They are subjecting candidates to longer and more interviews.

And they are using new interviewing techniques, some of which would make thumbscrews seem an attractive alternative.

Although no hire comes with a guarantee, many employers are "going the extra mile" to assure that they do not even *consider* someone they will quickly wish had never darkened their doors.

Simply put, despite the labor shortage, employers want to know a lot more about who they are hiring. If you have not taken a lot of time to uncover the "real you" hidden beneath the grades and athletics and clubs, don't worry. By the time you finish today's extended interview process, you'll be ready to lead a self-help seminar.

Hmmm. Maybe you have a good reason to be nervous after all.

Help Is In Your Hands

The purpose of this book is not to add to your anxiety, but to tell you how to conquer it. Of course, the best way to keep anxiety from hamstringing you during the interview is preparation. Know yourself. Know the company. And, if possible, know the interviewer. *Before* you're sitting in the reception area filling out an application.

This book will help you do that. It also will help you write effective letters that will get you in the door to show your stuff. It will give you a sneak preview of exactly what to expect on the interview. It will even tell you what your "interview suit" should look like.

Most importantly, this book will tell you in detail how to conduct yourself during every phase of the interview—how to make sure you're taking the right approach once you get to know the interviewer a bit and what you can expect to be asked.

It will tell you how to handle illegal or embarrassing questions, how to field the job offer, and how to make the most of salary discussions.

Who's In Charge Here?

Most of the advice in this book is pure common sense. But even the most seasoned job hunters who read it may well ask, "Now, why didn't I think of that?"

The reason is quite simple: Most job candidates think of the interview in completely the wrong way. They think of it as an interrogation. And see themselves as suspects, not as the key prospects they really are.

This book will help you approach the interview in a different way. It will show you that *you are,* to a very large degree, *in charge of the interview*. It will, I hope, convince you that you are there not only to sell the company on *you,* but to make sure that *you* are sold on *the company.*

Simply put, the interview is a two-way street. It is an exchange of information by two or more responsible adults. It is *not* a police lineup.

What's The Worst That Could Happen?

As we ready ourselves for particularly stressful situations—an important exam, a big date, *your first interview* —it's helpful to ask, "Well, what's the worst that can happen?" in an effort to put everything in perspective.

Here are some true-life interview stories:

- One candidate, about to be interviewed for the position of chief financial officer of a large company, showed up in the president's office wearing a jogging suit, hair matted and face reddened from a five-mile run to the interview.

- One man continually asked the director of human resources if he could phone his psychiatrist to make sure he was answering the questions correctly.

- A candidate at one company lay down on the floor through the entire interview, taking the hiring manager's advice to "relax" perhaps a bit too literally.

What's the worst that can happen? Sure, these candidates didn't get *those* jobs, but they eventually did go on to find employment elsewhere.

I'm sure that you won't do anything that foolish during your first interview. And, even if you do, what's the worst that can happen?

You'd just have to re-read this book.

Chapter 1

Getting To Know Them

The Importance of Company Research

Most people headed for their first job interview rival the most avid narcissists in the self-absorption department.

They've spent days giving their resumes the "right look" and taken hours selecting their outfits and making sure every strand of hair is in place.

And they have practiced, practiced, practiced—they're ready to talk for hours about themselves and the traits that will make them terrific employees.

Helpful. Useful. Even necessary. But if that's all *you* do before you walk through the door for your first interview, you have left out perhaps the most important step of all.

The best preparation for your first job interview involves looking far beyond the mirror. You must take the time to learn about the company for which you hope to work, the job for which you are interviewing, and, if possible, the interviewer.

Getting this information is often not particularly difficult, though it may well be time-consuming, but such detailed company research is probably the key step most first-time interviewers skip.

What Kind Of Salesperson Are You?

To understand the importance of pre-interview preparation, think of yourself as a salesperson. Would calling potential clients or customers without knowing anything about their businesses or how they could make use of your products impress you as an effective technique? Would selling them thousands of dollars of your product without knowing how well they were doing—whether they were even financially sound—make sense?

Of course not. Then why do so many candidates show up for job interviews with only the vaguest knowledge about the company, even though they are there to sell their most important product—themselves?

Virtually every interviewer will ask a candidate what questions he or she has about the company. This is not merely the interviewer's way of being nice. It is a very effective technique to gauge *your* interest in the company as the interviewer tries to determine the extent to which *the company* should be interested in you.

Of course, sharpening your sales pitch is not the only reason to research the company. You should do your homework to make sure that the company is one you would want to work for should you get the job. Otherwise, within weeks (or worse, days or hours!) of sliding behind your new desk, you'll wonder why you ever agreed to work there in the first place!

Starting Your Detective Work

The best place to start your investigation is your college placement office or library. Look for these reference tools:

- *The Career Directory Series* (The Career Press)
- *College Placement Directory* (Zimmerman & Lavine)

- *College Placement Annual* (College Placement Council)
- Dun & Bradstreet's various directories
- *F&S Index of Corporations and Industries*
- Fitch Corporations Manuals
- Moody's Manuals
- *MacRae's Bluebook*
- *Standard & Poor's Register of Corporations, Directors and Executives*
- *Thomas Register of American Companies*

These can all be invaluable sources of information. I recommend most highly the *F&S Index,* which lists published articles by industry and company. This will help you obtain objective information about the latest developments at a company and in an industry. It can help you find many articles that will arm you with terrific, up-to-date knowledge about the company, just the right kind of information that will help you impress an interviewer.

If your search through these valuable reference tools proves fruitless or only marginally productive, these other outside sources of information should help:

- The **Chamber of Commerce** in the community that's home to the company or division. How has the company been performing? Has it been growing or shrinking? How many people does it employ? How many did it employ in the community two years ago? Do people consider it a good place to work?

- **Business/industry associations.** Consult the *Encyclopaedia of Associations* (Gale Research) to find out the names of trade and professional organizations to which the company might belong. Ask a research or public relations representative the same questions you asked the chamber of commerce.

- *Executive, professional and technical placement agencies.* If you are getting the job interview through an agent, see how much you can learn about the prospective employer from him or her.

- *Business editors.* Turn the tables on the news media: Ask *them* the questions! A community newspaper's business reporter or editor will usually be the person most knowledgeable about local companies. They will know about developments at particular companies, how employees like working for them, how they are viewed by the community.

- *School alumni.* The college placement office, your fraternity/sorority or alumni association might be able to tell you about someone working at the company. Give him or her a call. Alumni are usually happy to help someone from the old school who's about to enter the job market.

- *Stock brokers/analysts.* If the company is public, it will have an investor relations representative who can tell you which brokers and analysts "follow the stock." This means that a representative of the brokerage has visited with the company, analyzed its industry, balance sheet, and management, and written a detailed report for investors. Call the brokerage and ask for a copy of the report. It will be objective, very revealing, and give you terrific material for impressing the interviewer.

- *Books.* There were a number of business books that hit the market during the 1980s which can help you get a better understanding of a company or an industry. Your library will have some of the titles dealing with well-known corporations. To find others, again, I recommend calling the trade associations.

Profiting From Inside Information

Once you've culled the outside—and probably more objective—sources of information, take a look at what the company tells the public about itself. Once you have the interview lined up, call the interviewer's secretary or the company's investor relations department to obtain the following:

- *Annual reports.* Mark Twain said that there are three kinds of lies—"lies, damned lies, and statistics"—and you'll find all of them in most annual reports. Read between the lines (and the lies) of the annual report to learn as much as you can about the company.

  It should tell you how the company's sales and profits have been increasing or decreasing over the past few years. It will tell you what the company's plans are for the year ahead. And it should give some indication of the health of the industry in which the company operates.

  In addition, it should indicate how the company feels about its employees. Note whether the company talks about accomplishments of particular employees. Does it have photos of people at work? Or does it stick strictly to "the numbers" and vague musings of the chairman?

- *Employee handbooks.* Be gutsy. Ask the company to send you a copy of this valuable document. At the very least, the handbook will tell you all about benefits, vacation time, salary review policies, and other items you might not want to ask about on the interview. It also should give you valuable insights into the company's attitude toward its employees.

- *Sales/marketing brochures.* Knowing about a company's products will help you determine whether you'd like to work for the organization and will give you terrific material upon which to base questions.

The Value Of Homework

I know of one candidate, a marketing major, who spent a great deal of time poring over the brochures from an aerospace contractor. During his initial interview, he stunned the recruiter by knowing so much about the company's guidance systems. In fact, the candidate relieved the interviewer of the task he hated to perform most— explaining the company's complicated technology.

What To Ask Campus Recruiters

Often the first contacts you will have with a company are the recruiters who come to harvest the best and brightest students from your graduating class.

When you meet with these representatives, don't be content to sit there and answer their questions. Make it your goal to find out information that will help *you* ease on down the interview road.

Ask about the company's products. What other students from your school has it hired in the past? How far have they gotten up the corporate ladder? Who will make the final hiring decision for the position in which you're interested?

Ask the recruiters, if they seem interested in you, to send you the annual reports, product brochures, and other materials mentioned above.

The Answers To Your Questions

Now that you know where to find information about prospective employers, here are specific questions for which you should be seeking equally specific answers:

- What are the company's leading products? What products will it be looking to introduce in the near future?

- What are the company's key markets? How strong are these markets?

- What are the prospects for growth and expansion? Will the company grow internally or through mergers and acquisitions?

- What rate of growth does the company project over the next few years?

- To what does the company attribute fluctuations in sales?

- Has the company "downsized" recently? What were the extent of these layoffs and early retirements?

- Do reductions of staff seem likely in the near future?

Finding Out About The Interviewer

Now comes the toughest detective work of all—finding out a little bit about the person who will be firing the questions at you. This is not as important for your meeting with the recruiter in the Human Resources Department. But it is crucial for your meeting with the hiring manager.

Let's face it, in the initial interview, you'll have perhaps forty-five minutes to convince someone that you're the best candidate for the job. It probably will help to know which are the right buttons to push to get the interviewer to notice—and remember—you.

Tim, a business associate of mine, asked the Personnel Department to send him as many back issues as it could of the company newsletter when he was preparing to be interviewed for an open position. He then devoured the newsletters, studying everything from the birth and wedding announcements to the opening letter from the president of the company.

This enabled him to begin questions like this: "I've read that your company has recently installed a computer-integrated manufacturing system..."

He also learned that the company had been increasing its sales volume substantially, which led him to ask some informed questions about the company's successes. He told me that he could sense how impressed the interviewer was that he had done so much research on the company.

But that was just the start of Tim's use of his research. The newsletters told him that his interviewer, Mr. Marty, had been with the company for twenty years and worked his way up from a lower-level job in the distribution department.

The biography in the newsletter also indicated that Marty was an avid bird-watcher.

Tim did a little bit of research into bird-watching—just enough to make some intelligent comments about the pictures of winged creatures on Marty's walls—and framed questions that demonstrated a willingness to follow a career path similar to the one his prospective boss had.

One of your key goals on the interview is to stand out in bold relief from the other candidates for the position. Tim's efforts clearly helped him do just that.

Showing Your Stuff
Without Showing Off

The old saying, "If you've got it, flaunt it," is, in some ways, bad advice when it comes to interviewing for that job you want.

While you'll definitely want to demonstrate that you've prepared for this interview, have researched the company thoroughly and prepared a list of informed questions, avoid overdoing it. Don't try to cram into the interview every last scrap of knowledge about the company you've been able to glean in your research.

Flaunting your research will have two very negative consequences:

1. You will sound like a stock analyst's report that's been wired for sound.

2. You will probably show up the interviewer somewhere along the line. Odds are, the interviewer didn't read the annual report the night before your appointment, so he or she won't be as familiar with its details as *you* are. *Don't embarrass the interviewer!*

The best thing to do—and you'll read this throughout the book—is to relax and be yourself. If you have, indeed, done a lot of research on the company, that fact will become apparent in the type of questions you ask and some of the answers you give.

Work your research into your conversation with the interviewer deftly and as unobtrusively as possible. Don't hit him over the head with the encyclopedia of ABC Widget.

Two other important points to remember:

1. You cannot learn anything if you are doing all the talking. You don't just want to sell yourself

to the company during your job interview. You want to give the company every opportunity to sell itself to *you*. Don't take up the interviewer's time showing off your knowledge. He'll learn little about the real you, and you'll learn even less from him.

2. People are more likely to hire, or recommend for hire, people they like. Not too many people like showoffs who enjoy hearing themselves talk.

Learn More During The Interview

Solid research also will prepare you to learn everything you want about the company before the conclusion of the interview. It will help you frame questions that will turn the interview into a two-way street, a learning experience for you as well as your inquisitors.

If you've read that the organization is family-owned, find out how this might affect your prospects for promotion. If you've heard it has a tuition-reimbursement plan, find out how and when you can participate in it. If the newsletter reported that an employee opinion poll had been taken, discreetly ask for some of the results.

Asking about some of these areas can be rather delicate. We'll talk about how to frame your questions (so they are taken as brilliant indications of your interest and *not* insulting examples of your insensitivity!) in Chapter 9.

Chapter 2

Getting The Interview

Homework Really Does Pay Off

Although nobody likes doing it, homework does have its payoffs. Especially in the job hunt. From the research you doggedly pursued on each prospective employer, you should have learned several important things:

- What the company is looking for in its employees.
- Who the hiring manager is and what type of people he or she usually hires.
- What the company's key products and markets are.
- Whether or not the company has hired employees from your school, with your degree, and how they've fared.
- Why you might enjoy working for the organization.

All of this information will prove invaluable to you, not only during the interview, but in helping you *get* the interview in the first place.

Who Can You Turn To?

Whether you're answering a classified advertisement or launching an all-out direct-mail assault on the best companies in the industry you've chosen, you'll want to *write to the hiring manager, not the personnel department.*

The reason is quite simple: Personnel departments usually have little idea about what the hiring manager really wants in a job applicant. The more technical or specialized the field, the truer this statement.

I've known of a personnel director who recommended a candidate for whom English was a second—and not very *good*—language for the top editorial post on a major association magazine.

Another passed along a candidate that got 55 (out of 100) on a spelling test for a proofreading position.

Still another recommended someone whose resume was filled with rather obvious or easily discovered lies for a vice president-finance position.

Why would you trust your fate to such people?

At many organizations, hiring managers make it a point to go around the personnel department—bringing candidates in, interviewing them, and only *then* passing them along so personnel can make sure all of the "i's" are dotted and "t's" crossed on their applications.

Make it easier for the hiring manager to do just that. Get in touch with him or her yourself.

What To Put In That Winning Letter

The letter on p. 25 is by Gregory Wright, a candidate who is about to get out of college and stride tentatively into the workaday world. Let's take a look at several of the key components of this letter:

1. It's typed on the applicant's letterhead. A nice— and professional—touch. Design and print *your* own letterhead and envelopes. Use a quality letter stock in off-white or buff, light blue or light grey. (Your resume should be printed on the same stock.)

   Also note that the typeface used is not too fancy. It is a common, readable style, not some old-English script that requires a Ph.D. in Chaucer to translate.

2. It addresses by name and title the manager with the authority to hire him. (Naturally Greg had the good sense and professionalism to triple-check the spelling of both the name and title!)

3. The first paragraph immediately states the reason Greg wrote the letter. It indicates the specific job or type of work for which he was applying and where (or from whom) he learned about the opening.

4. The second and third paragraphs contain his sales pitch. Tell the hiring manager why he or she should consider you for the job, what you offer the company, why you deserve an interview.

5. Liven things up a bit. Refer to your resume and tell the hiring manager a little more about yourself. But don't overdo it.

   Let's face it, as a college student, you don't have *that* much to sell to a prospective employer. It's important to mention such things as internships, but don't oversell them.

6. Mention the name of the company and, if convenient, some fact that you know about it. This

will make your letter look unlike so many of the form letters job seekers send out.

7. This letter provides absolutely no information that is not related to the job. If a manager wants to learn more about you, he or she will make an attempt do so during the interview. But he or she is probably *not* interested in slogging through a lot of extraneous information in a letter. As Sergeant Friday would say on *Dragnet*, "Just the facts, ma'am."

8. It's important to keep the letter to one page. Anything more might lead some managers to just toss it unread. (Yes, it's a jungle out there, and you're pretty much the proverbial supper to its hungry inhabitants.)

A couple of other cautions: Always type, never handwrite, the manager's name and address on the envelope, no matter how inconvenient your word processor or typewriter makes this process. And, if you have a summer job, *do not* send the letter through the company's postage meter. It makes you look like a petty crook. Use your own stamp.

You've Got It Covered

Why is the cover letter so important?

Well, we've established that it is best for you to apply for your job with the hiring manager. A letter addressed to that person will be read, particularly if you mark the envelope "personal and confidential."

Even if the manager asked his secretary to screen *all* of his mail, that person will treat a personal letter, which they will pass on to the manager, differently than someone's resume, which they also will pass on—to Personnel.

Gregory L. Wright
104 HIGHLAND AVENUE
YORKTOWN HEIGHTS, NY 11345
914/555-1237

September 15, 1991

Mr. Robert Carr
Vice President, Sales
ABC Sportswear
1315 Broadway
New York, NY 10036

Dear Mr. Carr:

The sales trainee position at ABC Sportswear briefly described in your June 23 *New York Times* advertisement is very appealing to me. Please accept this letter and the attached resume as application for this opening.

While majoring in business (with a marketing minor) at Wallace State, I worked on a number of special projects that helped me develop some of the skills mentioned in your ad. Specifically, I gained a great deal of knowledge about budgeting, telemarketing and account analysis

As a summer intern for Reebok, I was able to refine some of my skills as I worked with the promotion department to develop a sales-call management system. My internship at Shaw Electronics gave me experience in helping establish a data base marketing program.

I would like to meet with you at your convenience to discuss this position and my qualifications for it in more detail. I learned a great deal about ABC from your campus recruiter Nick Deane and think it would be a terrific place to work.

Thank you for your time. I look forward to meeting with you.

Sincerely yours,

Gregory Wright

Okay, Sometimes You Should Use Personnel

I have stressed the importance of writing your letter to the real decision maker, the hiring manager. However, it sometimes *is* advisable to contact the personnel department, especially given your current lack of experience.

If you have targeted a particular company, but are not sure whether any job openings exist, get in touch with the Director of Personnel (or Human Resources), again, by name. Tell him or her the reasons that you'd like to work for the company, the positions you think you'd be qualified for, and something about yourself and your accomplishments.

A former colleague of mine, whom I'll call Charlie, wanted to work in the public relations department of Wonder Drug., Inc., one of the large pharmaceutical houses in New Jersey. His reasons: The company had consistently been cited in business magazines and textbooks as one of the best run in America, and it spent more on developing new products than any other company in the industry.

Charlie "networked" like the dickens. He asked everyone *he* knew if *they* knew anyone at Wonder Drug. Finally, he came across someone whose friend's father, a Mr. Jones, worked there. He got in touch with the friend and asked if he could call his dad. Mr. Jones was delighted to be contacted. Charlie asked Mr. Jones if he knew the head of the public relations department and whether he knew of any openings there.

The man did, in fact, know the head of P.R., but wasn't sure about openings. My friend asked if he could use Mr. Jones's name in a letter, and Mr. Jones, after spending some time with Charlie, gracefully said yes.

Charlie practically ran to his typewriter and composed the letter on p. 27.

Charles Goett

7 Lobell Court, West Orange, N.J. 07009
201/748-2098

August 1, 1991

Mr. David Basting
Director of Public Relations
Wonder Drug, Inc.
One Wonder Plaza
Harmon Meadow, N.J. 07123

Dear Mr. Basting:

I am writing at the suggestion of your colleague, Robert Jones, to inquire about possible openings in the Public Relations department at Wonder Drug, Inc. Mr. Jones mentioned that your company does hire entry-level people in your department.

Mr. Basting, it has been my dream to work in the public relations department of a prestigious company such as yours. More specifically, for the past few months I've developed a keen desire to work for Wonder Drug. Everything I've read about your company in business magazines and leading management books convinces me that yours is one of the most well run, innovative, and decent companies in the world. I'm sure it is an honor to publicize many of the products developed at such a company.

And I'm the right person for any openings you might have now or in the near future. While taking a double major in business and journalism at City State, I worked in the school's publicity office. During my summers, I interned for Engulf & Devour Public Relations, writing and trying to secure placements for releases on companies such as Bon Vivant and Alia Industries.

I would like to meet with you to discuss possible openings and my qualifications in more detail. I will call you in a week to see if we can set up an appointment.

Thank you for your time. I look forward to meeting with you.

Sincerely yours,

Charles Goett

The Follow-Up Phone Call

You've sealed your message in the bottle and thrown it out to sea. The optimists among you will expect their telephones to ring off the hook with job offers within two days. Pessimists will expect to hear nothing.

Unfortunately, in most cases, the pessimists are right. When your letter produces nothing, you probably will feel depressed. You just can't *believe* that some lucky company out there has been given the chance to *hire* you and has not jumped at it. It's probably unrealistic for you to feel quite so surprised. After all, that company you're interested in working for *has* been thriving without you for some time.

What do you do? Well, to borrow a phrase from sales-motivation speakers, "Make it happen!" And the way to make it happen, as every salesperson knows, is to follow your letter up with a phone call.

I suggest waiting to call until a week after you've posted your letter. However, I advise against calling on Monday or Friday, first thing in the morning, toward 5:00 in the evening, or during the 12:00 to 2:00 lunch shift. In other words, place your call between 10:00 and 12:00 or between 2:30 and 4:00 on Tuesday, Wednesday, or Thursday.

Odds are you won't get through to the Bastings and Carrs of the world. You'll get secretaries, receptionists, message desks, and, increasingly these days, voice-mail or answering machines. Here's the way a typical conversation might proceed:

Secretary: *Mr. Basting's office.*

You: *Hello, I'm wondering if Mr. Basting is available. My name is Charles Goett.*

S: *What is this about, Mr. Goett?*

Y: *I sent a letter to Mr. Basting on August 1. Do you know if he's received it?*

S: *What was it regarding?*

Y: *I was writing to inquire about possible openings in your department.*

S: *Well, I don't know of any openings at this time. But I'll see to it that Mr. Basting gets your message.*

Y: *When do you expect that I'll hear from him?*

S: *Well, he's been very busy, so I can't answer that, but I will see to it that he does get your message.*

Y: *I appreciate that. Have a nice day.*

Despite the fact that you're being stonewalled, maintain a pleasant tone during such conversations. In fact, as any good telemarketer will tell you, it helps if you smile while you're speaking on the phone. Smiling actually improves the tone of your delivery.

If you've cited a "network" connection in your letter to Mr. Basting or if your skills are a match, you'll probably hear back from him. If you don't hear back within a week or so, or by the time the secretary told you that he might call back, call again. See if the secretary can assure you that your letter arrived.

Remember, *always* be pleasant on the phone. A secretary or assistant who takes a dislike to you can be lethal to your hopes of landing a job.

"Don't Call Us..."

If your second phone call produces nothing, you'll know that you're in a "don't-call-us-we'll-call-you" situation. It's probably best to give up unless you have another connection that you can exploit.

If you receive a letter acknowledging receipt of your resume, but rejecting your application, follow up with a note thanking the person for responding and asking him or her to keep you in mind for any future openings.

The letter should read something like the one on p. 31—it shows that you are attentive, courteous and somewhat aggressive. It also helps ensure that the only reason you didn't hear from Basting is because your letter scored a quick two points in his secretary's "circular file."

What If They *Do* Call You

If, on the other hand, someone calls you with a positive response to your letter, stay calm—and don't drop the phone!

In fact, you should be at least somewhat prepared for this to happen. An increasing number of companies are pre-screening candidates on the telephone to save time and reduce recruitment costs.

The hiring manager or a representative from the personnel department will have a battery of questions for you. We will discuss the content of these questions in the next chapter. Relax. You'll be ready.

If you do secure the interview, follow up with a confirming note. It should read like the letter on p. 32.

Well, the easy part is over. You've secured your chance to interview for a job. You've done your homework on the company. You've written the best letter of your life. And you've sold yourself in writing and over the telephone.

But that's only the beginning. Now you must prepare and rehearse for your interview and endure what for many is an emotional seesaw between hope and dread. However, the following chapters can help assure that that emotional seesaw ends up being a joy ride.

Charles Goett

7 Lobell Court, West Orange, N.J. 07009
201/748-2098

August 10, 1991

Mr. David Basting
Director of Public Relations
Wonder Drug, Inc.
One Wonder Plaza
Harmon Meadow, N.J. 07123

Dear Mr. Basting:

Naturally, I was disappointed that there are no positions open for me at this time at Wonder Drug, Inc. As I indicated in my letter of August 1, I have long been an admirer of your company and thought that my skills in marketing would make me a valuable contributor.

I am enclosing another copy of my resume that I hope you will keep on file in the event that a position opens for which you think I am qualified.

I look forward to hearing from you some time in the future.

Sincerely yours,

Charles Goett

Charles Goett

7 Lobell Court, West Orange, N.J. 07009
201/748-2098

August 10, 1991

Mr. David Basting
Director of Public Relations
Wonder Drug, Inc.
One Wonder Plaza
Harmon Meadow, N.J. 07123

Dear Mr. Basting:

I am looking forward to meeting with you on August 15 at 9:30 a.m. to discuss the opening in your department. I am very excited by the chance to work for your company as assistant director of solid waste management.

Thank you for the opportunity.

Sincerely yours,

Charles Goett

Chapter 3

Developing A Personal Inventory

Just Who Do You Think You Are?

What constantly astounds personnel people about college students going for their first job is how unprepared they are. So many of them (you), these professionals tell me, think they can just "wing it" that the majority of first-time job candidates usually end up tongue-tied over the simplest and most common interview questions.

To begin preparing for the interview process, let's start with the hardest of all interview questions, one that's been known to confound the people interviewing *you* when they were interviewed for *their* jobs!

Double Jeopardy

The $64,000 job interview question is: *How would you describe yourself?*

When asked, this question all too often produces a deep silence and a great deal of eye shifting. A typical candidate searches his brain frantically for the right answer to this seemingly innocuous question.

But the question is not at all innocuous. It can "make or break" the job interview. It *should* be seen as a wonderful opportunity, often the only time during the whole process that you will be given *carte blanche*, a chance to say anything you want to sell yourself. It's your 15 minutes of fame. Your shot on Carson.

Unfortunately, most of you will wind up sounding more like Jackie Gleason's "chef of the future" on *The Honeymooners,* hemming and hawing as you try to back out of the room, knocking a chair over on the way. Memorable exit. No job.

That's because most candidates, and most people in general, don't really know the answer to the question, "How would you describe yourself," or, more simply put, "Who Are You?"

Gosh, I Never Thought Of That

They don't know the answer because they've probably never thought about the question—*really* thought about it. Most of us are uncomfortable with introspection. And, let's face it, the days immediately before and after graduation seem like the wrong time for contemplating one's navel.

However, it *is* essential for you to take time out *now* to get to know yourself better. You might be getting through school with flying colors, but you'll flunk in the job market unless you take time to perform a personal inventory.

Information At Your Fingertips

During the interview, it will be helpful to have as much knowledge about yourself memorized and rehearsed as possible. Take some time to assemble all of the following information. (Keeping separate folders with pertinent data, citations, notes, etc. is an excellent idea.)

Employment Records

Details on every part-time or full-time job you've held, including:

- Each employer's name, address and telephone number
- Name of supervisor
- Exact dates worked
- Approximate numbers of hours per week
- Specific duties and responsibilities
- Specific skills utilized
- Accomplishments, honors
- Copies of awards, letters of recommendation

Volunteer Activities

Just because you weren't paid for a specific job—stuffing envelopes for the local Republican candidate, running a car wash to raise money for the homeless, manning a drug hot-line—doesn't mean that it wasn't significant or that you won't want to include it on your resume. So keep the same detailed notes on these volunteer activities as you have on the jobs you've held:

- Each organization's name, address and telephone number
- Name of supervisor
- Exact dates worked
- Approximate number of hours per week
- Specific duties and responsibilities
- Specific skills utilized
- Accomplishments, honors
- Copies of awards, letters of recommendation

Extracurricular Activities

List all sports, clubs or other activities in which you've participated, either inside or outside school. For each, you should include:

- Name of activity/club/group
- Office(s) held
- Purpose of club/activity
- Specific duties/responsibilities
- Achievements, accomplishments, awards

Honors And Awards

Even if some of these honors are previously listed, specific data on every honor or award you receive should be kept, including, of course, the award itself! Keep the following information in your awards folder:

- Award name
- Date and from whom received
- What it was for
- Any pertinent details

Military Records

Complete military history, if pertinent, including:

- Dates of service
- Final rank awarded
- Duties and responsibilities
- All citations and awards
- Details on specific training and/or special schooling
- Skills developed
- Specific accomplishments

At the end of this chapter, I have prepared eight *Data Input Sheets* (with multiple copies of some, where needed). The first six cover employment, volunteer work, education, activities and awards. The last two—covering military service and language skills—are important if, of course, they apply to you.

Here are some pointers on how to fill out these all-important Data Sheets:

- *Employment Data Input Sheet:* You will need to record the basic information—employer's name, address and phone number, dates of employment and your supervisor's name—for your own files anyway. It may be an important addition to your networking list and will be necessary should you be asked to supply a reference list.

  Duties should be a one- or two-sentence paragraph describing what you did on this job. For example, if you worked as a hostess in a restaurant, this section might read: "Responsible for the delivery of 250 meals at dinner time and the supervision of 20 waiters and busboys. Coordinated reservations. Responsible for check and payment verification."

  Skills should enumerate specific capabilities necessary for the job or developed through it.

  If you achieved *specific results*—"developed new filing system," "collected over $5,000 in previously assumed bad debt," "instituted award-winning art program," etc.—or *received any award, citation or other honor*—"named Employee of the Month three times," "received Citation for Innovation," etc.—make sure you list these.

  Prepare one employment data sheet for each job you have held, no matter how short the job

(yes, summer jobs count) or how limited you
may think it is. Though I've included three
blank Input Sheets for your use, you may need to
prepare more.

- *Volunteer Work Data Input Sheet:* Treat any
  volunteer work, no matter how basic or short
  (one day counts!), as if it were a job and record
  the same information. In both cases, it is especially important to note specific duties and
  responsibilities, skills required or developed and
  any accomplishments or achievements you can
  point to as evidence of your success.

- *Educational Data Input Sheets:* If you're in
  college, omit details on high school. If you're a
  graduate student, list details on both graduate
  and undergraduate coursework. If you have not
  yet graduated, list your anticipated date of graduation. If more than a year away, indicate the
  numbers of credits earned through the most
  recent semester to be completed.

- *Activities Data Input Sheet:* This is where to list
  your participation in the Student Government,
  Winter Carnival Press Committee, Math Club,
  Ski Patrol, etc., plus sports teams and/or any
  participation in community or church groups.
  Make sure you indicate if you were elected to any
  positions in clubs, groups or on teams.

- *Awards And Honors Data Input Sheet:* List
  awards and honors from your school (prestigious high school awards can still be included
  here, even if you're in graduate school), community groups, church groups, clubs, etc.

- *Military Service Data Input Sheet:* Many useful
  skills are learned in the armed forces. A military stint often hastens the maturation process,

making you a more attractive candidate. So if you have served in the military, make sure you have the details ready to discuss.

- *Language Data Input Sheet:* An extremely important section for those of you with a real proficiency in a second language. And *do* make sure you have at least conversational fluency in the language(s) you list. One year of college French doesn't count, but if you spent a year studying abroad, you probably are fluent or near-fluent. Such a talent could be invaluable, especially if you hope to work in the international arena.

While you should use these forms to summarize all of the data you have collected, do not throw away any of the specific information—report cards, transcripts, citations, etc.—just because it is recorded on these sheets. Keep *all* records in your files; you'll never know when you'll need them again!

What's It All About?

These forms now contain a great deal of information, but all they really reveal about you is what you've done and where you've been. Take some time to think over your personal history these forms contain, using the following questions as a guide:

1. What achievements did you have in school or in your brief work experience? Which made you the proudest? Why? How and why were you able to score these successes? What bearing will these achievements have on your success in your career? Why?

2. What failures in your life do you think about most often? Why did they happen? Have you done anything to keep them from occurring again? Have you learned from your mistakes? How?

3. How do you interact with authority figures— bosses, teachers, parents? Do these interactions show the promise of success or failure with bosses you'll have down the line? How?

This exercise will be most effective if you write down your answers. Because it's for your eyes only, you needn't be concerned about producing beautiful prose, or, for that matter, even complete sentences. The only important thing is honesty.

Now That *That's* Over With

If you are being brutally frank and honest, this exercise has probably told you things about yourself you never realized, and it's probably been difficult. But don't think you're out of the woods yet. We have to get to know you a little better.

Again, get a piece of paper and start writing. Here are some more tough questions:

1. What games and sports do you enjoy? What does the way you play these games say about you? Are you overly competitive? Do you give up too easily? Are you a good loser or a bad winner? Do you rise to a challenge or back away?

2. What kind of friends do you tend to have? Do you look only for people that are very similar to you? Do you tolerate differences? Do you look for syco- phants that will laugh at all of your jokes? What are the things that have caused you to break up friendships? What does this say about you?

3. If you were to ask a group of friends and acquaintances to describe you, what adjectives would they use? List all of them. Why would people describe you in this way? Are there specific behaviors, skills, achievements, failures that lead to the use of these adjectives? What are they?

The Best And The Worst

Now, look over all that you've written down so far and distill it into several lists with the following headings:

- Strongest skills.
- Greatest areas of knowledge.
- Strongest parts of my personality.
- The things I do best.
- Skills that I should develop to do well in my career.
- Areas of my personality that I should improve.

You will be amazed at the results of this exercise if you take the time to do it correctly, and, again, if you are brutally honest with yourself. It should help you realize things about yourself that you never knew, or, more accurately, that you never *knew* you knew.

Once More, With Feeling

I urge you to do this exercise when there is no imminent need to use the information—that is, *now,* before you have your first interview scheduled. Then, when you have your first interview set up, take out your lists along with a clean sheet of paper and answer the following questions:

1. What in my personal inventory will convince this employer that I deserve the position for which I am going to interview?

2. What are the strengths, achievements, skills, and areas of knowledge that make me most qualified for this position? What in my background should separate me from the pack of candidates for the position?

3. What weaknesses should I admit to, if asked about them, and how will I indicate that I will or have improved them?

A Little Knowledge Is A Dangerous Thing

The failure to perform a personal inventory will mean that you are not fully prepared for your interview. Knowing yourself a little better, on the other hand, will help build your self confidence. You'll know that you are going into the interview prepared to answer the toughest questions the inquisitor can throw at you—those about yourself.

I hope that these first three chapters have convinced you of the importance of doing your homework before the interview.

The next few chapters will demonstrate why that homework is *essential*.

EMPLOYMENT DATA INPUT SHEET

Employer Name: _____

Address: _____

Address: _____

Phone: _____

Dates of Employment: _____ to _____

Hours Per Week: _____ Salary/Pay: _____

Supervisor's Name & Title: _____

Duties: _____

_____

_____

Skills Utilized: _____

_____

_____

Accomplishments/Honors/Awards: _____

_____

_____

Other Important Information: _____

_____

_____

EMPLOYMENT DATA INPUT SHEET

Employer Name:_____

Address:_____

Address:_____

Phone:_____

Dates of Employment: _____ to _____

Hours Per Week:_____   Salary/Pay:_____

Supervisor's Name & Title:_____

Duties:_____

_____

_____

Skills Utilized:_____

_____

_____

Accomplishments/Honors/Awards:_____

_____

_____

Other Important Information:_____

_____

_____

_____

EMPLOYMENT DATA INPUT SHEET

Employer Name:_____

Address:_____

Address:_____

Phone:_____

Dates of Employment: _____ to _____

Hours Per Week:_____ Salary/Pay:_____

Supervisor's Name & Title:_____

Duties:_____

_____

_____

Skills Utilized:_____

_____

_____

Accomplishments/Honors/Awards:_____

_____

_____

Other Important Information:_____

_____

_____

VOLUNTEER WORK DATA INPUT SHEET

Organization Name:_____

Address:_____

Address:_____

Phone:_____   Hours Per Week: _____

Dates of Activity:_____

Supervisor's Name & Title: _____

Duties:_____

_____

_____

Skills Utilized:_____

_____

_____

Accomplishments/Honors/Awards: _____

_____

_____

Other Important Information:_____

_____

_____

_____

VOLUNTEER WORK DATA INPUT SHEET

Organization Name: _____

Address: _____

Address: _____

Phone: _____   Hours Per Week: _____

Dates of Activity: _____

Supervisor's Name & Title: _____

Duties: _____

_____

_____

Skills Utilized: _____

_____

_____

Accomplishments/Honors/Awards: _____

_____

_____

Other Important Information: _____

_____

_____

_____

HIGH SCHOOL DATA INPUT SHEET

School Name:_____

Address:_____

Address:_____

Phone:_____ Years Attended:_____

Major Studies:_____

GPA/Class Rank:_____

Honors:_____

Important Courses:_____

_____

OTHER SCHOOL DATA INPUT SHEET

School Name:_____

Address:_____

Address:_____

Phone:_____ Years Attended:_____

Major Studies:_____

GPA/Class Rank:_____

Honors:_____

Important Courses:_____

COLLEGE DATA INPUT SHEET

College:_____

Address:_____

Phone:_____ Years Attended:_____

Degrees Earned:_____ Major:_____

Minor:_____ Honors:_____

_____

Important Courses:_____

_____

_____

GRADUATE SCHOOL DATA INPUT SHEET

College:_____

Address:_____

Phone:_____ Years Attended:_____

Degrees Earned:_____ Major:_____

Minor:_____ Honors:_____

_____

Important Courses:_____

_____

ACTIVITIES DATA INPUT SHEET

Club/Activity: _____

Office(s) Held: _____

Description of Participation: _____

_____

Duties/Responsibilities: _____

_____

_____

Club/Activity: _____

Office(s) Held: _____

Description of Participation: _____

_____

Duties/Responsibilities: _____

_____

_____

Club/Activity: _____

Office(s) Held: _____

Description of Participation: _____

_____

Duties/Responsibilities: _____

_____

_____

ACTIVITIES DATA INPUT SHEET

Club/Activity: _____

Office(s) Held: _____

Description of Participation: _____

_____

Duties/Responsibilities: _____

_____

_____

Club/Activity: _____

Office(s) Held: _____

Description of Participation: _____

_____

Duties/Responsibilities: _____

_____

_____

Club/Activity: _____

Office(s) Held: _____

Description of Participation: _____

_____

Duties/Responsibilities: _____

_____

AWARDS & HONORS DATA INPUT SHEET

Name of Award, Citation, Etc.: _____

From Whom Received: _____

Date: _____   Significance: _____

_____

Other Pertinent Information: _____

_____

_____

Name of Award, Citation, Etc.: _____

From Whom Received: _____

Date: _____   Significance: _____

_____

Other Pertinent Information: _____

_____

_____

Name of Award, Citation, Etc.: _____

From Whom Received: _____

Date: _____   Significance: _____

_____

Other Pertinent Information: _____

_____

_____

MILITARY SERVICE DATA INPUT SHEET

Branch:_____

Rank (at Discharge):_____

Dates of Service:_____

. Duties & Responsibilities: _____

_____

_____

_____

Special Training and/or School Attended: _____

_____

_____

_____

_____

Citations, Awards, etc.:_____

_____

_____

Specific Accomplishments:_____

_____

_____

_____

LANGUAGE DATA INPUT SHEET

Language:_____

☐ Read   ☐ Write   ☐ Converse

Background (number of years studied, travel, etc.): _____

_____

_____

_____

Language:_____

☐ Read   ☐ Write   ☐ Converse

Background (number of years studied, travel, etc.): _____

_____

_____

_____

Language:_____

☐ Read   ☐ Write   ☐ Converse

Background (number of years studied, travel, etc.): _____

_____

_____

_____

_____

Chapter 4

Not The Spanish Inquisition!

What To Expect During Your First Interview

For employers, interviewing has made the transition from art to science.

A long-time subscriber to journals for personnel *(aka human resources)* executives, I've lately seen a plethora of articles extolling the virtues of such things as "database interviews," "situational interviews," and "stress (confrontational) interviews."

While these techniques each have their own nuances, they have been developed with one goal in mind: to more accurately and reliably measure how a candidate will perform on the job if hired.

Test-Tube Babies

Like scientists, interviewers are now expected to gather similar types of information on all the specimens they study—information that can be measured, quantified, and more easily and accurately compared. In fact, sometimes it seems as if quantification has replaced *qualification* in the hiring process.

The reasons are not as much Orwellian as economic. The "cost of hire"—the amount of money it takes to land a suitable candidate for a job—has escalated dramatically and will continue to increase as a result of the baby bust and the much ballyhooed shrinkage of the work force.

In addition, lawsuits against employers for wrongful discharge and other employment-related causes have increased exponentially over the past decade, making it more important for companies to hire people they (hope they) won't want to get rid of.

And, last but not least, for companies in our new Service Economy, the human resource is unquestionably the most valuable in their inventories.

Translation: Interviews Will Be Tougher

Not to make you more nervous than you probably already are, but for all of these reasons, interviewing is going to get tougher and tougher for job candidates at *all* levels of experience. You probably will have to go through more interviews than your predecessors—whatever job you are after, whatever your level of expertise—as well as tests designed to measure your honesty, intelligence, mental health and blood toxicity. (Employers seem to feel there's nothing worse than entry-level people on drugs, whatever your profession.)

The good news is that most of the newest interviewing techniques are being practiced by staffers in personnel departments—they are usually the only ones who have the time to read about these new techniques.

So, this chapter is designed to help you fly over the first hurdle on the track to your new job.

The Screening Interview

If you are going for a job at a mid-size or large company (any organization of more than about 250 employees), your first interview will often be with an employment or staffing manager in the personnel department.

More and more often, this interview is taking candidates by surprise. Why? Because many companies have begun conducting the initial screening interview by phone in an effort to save time and/or do more with less staff.

Therefore, since this will probably not be scheduled in advance, you must begin preparing for the telephone interview as soon as you send out your resumes and letters.

"I'll Get It"

The scene could go something like this: You're sitting at home having your orange juice on a warm summer day three weeks after graduation. The phone rings. You saunter over to answer it, casting sidelong glances at the headlines on the morning newspaper and scratching your stomach.

"Hello," you groan.

"Good morning," says the almost too chipper voice on the other end. *"This is Molly Ackroyd of ABC Widget. I'm looking for Joseph Lerman.*

"Speaking."

"Oh, hello. May I call you Joseph? You applied for our opening in the solid waste management department, and I'm calling to ask you some preliminary questions."

You're about to freeze. You gulp almost audibly. Your head swims in a rush of adrenaline. You begin looking for a way out. You consider saying, *"Oh, you want* Joseph Lerman. *I'm afraid he's not here right now. Can I take a message?"*

But you think better of it. and it's a good thing. After all, on the other end of the phone is not a great white shark, but Molly Ackroyd, recruitment manager at ABC Widget. Let's take a look at who she is and why she's calling you.

Joe Friday Again

Molly is a lower-level person in the personnel department who has been trained in some fairly basic interview techniques. Odds are that she hasn't been out of college much longer than you, and she has only a bare-bones idea of the duties and responsibilities of the position for which you've applied.

Her job has a rather simple goal: reduce the number of bona fide candidates for an opening before any of them get a chance to even walk in the door.

After you've gotten through the preliminaries with Molly, her end of the conversation will follow a script—she will be asking questions to see if you have the easily quantifiable qualifications for the position—the right degree, command of the English language, the right types of internships, willingness to relocate, whatever.

Primarily, Molly will be trying to determine if you've been truthful on your resume.

The interview will also be somewhat qualitative: How well have you responded to her surprise phone call? And how quickly did you recover from the shock? Do you exhibit sufficient enthusiasm for the position? Do you exhibit any obvious emotional disturbances? How articulate are you? How energetic? How prepared?

Should she or anybody else at Widget go out on a limb and actually recommend you for a *job?*

Okay, You Know What Molly Wants

So let her have it.

"Oh, Ms. Ackroyd, I'm so glad you called. What can I do for you this morning?"

You've shown enthusiasm and a willingness to be co-operative. Since Molly might have 25 of these calls to do today, she'll be very grateful to you for making her job easier and more pleasant.

Remember, the telephone interview is a screening *out,* not a screening *in* process. Molly is trying to *reduce* the number of in-person interviews she, her supervisor, and the hiring manager will have to conduct.

In other words, Molly desperately wants to scratch *24* of the (25) candidates she calls today off her list. In order to beat *these* odds:

- Make it easy for Molly to get hold of you or leave messages. Buy an answering machine if there is any time during business hours that your phone might not be answered.

- Be cheerful and enthusiastic without being phony about it. Remember to smile while you're speaking on the phone.

- Be prepared. Keep a copy of your resume and cover letter and some basic facts about ABC Widget and the other companies you've applied to right by the telephone.

- Stay in control. If you don't have documents near the phone, if you're in your underwear and the doorbell has just rung, ask Molly to hold on a few seconds or offer to call her right back. Do it calmly and don't think you'll put her off. She knows she's caught you by surprise.

- Rephrase Molly's questions and repeat them back
to her. This will give you time to think about your
reply. For example:

  *"Please tell me a little bit about your in-
  ternship at XYZ Dump."*

  *"Ah, my internship last summer at XYX?
  That was a terrific experience for me. I learned a
  great deal about solid waste management. For
  instance..."*

  This is a means of "warming up" for your
  reply, or remembering those answers I hope you
  have rehearsed before now (see Chapter 7).

- Make sure you ascertain the correct spelling of
Molly's name, her complete title and the address
of the company office she works in. You should
follow up the telephone interview with a letter
thanking her for calling and reaffirming your
interest in the position.

- Don't volunteer anything. The telephone interviewer is out to get facts and assess the truthful-
ness of your application. Something you might
volunteer could be a reason for rejection. If you
abruptly switched majors, entered and left graduate school, resigned from an internship or part-
time job, let Molly ask before you tell. Tell the
truth when she *does* ask, but don't feel the need to
unburden yourself if she *doesn't*.

The Live And In-Person
Screening Interview

Let's face it, the deck is stacked against you when Molly
calls. She wants to speak once and *only* once to as many
people that day as possible. It's more difficult to put your

best foot forward over the telephone. And, if the company is not in a remote location, it probably is using telephone screening because so many apparently qualified candidates applied for the position. Yes, that's right. You're not the only one to hear about that terrific job at ABC Widget. In fact, you're one of 200!

On the other hand, the live screening interview gives you a better chance to make a good impression (we'll discuss that more in the next chapter), and probably is an indication that there is a relatively small cadre of candidates or that your application is held in at least relatively high regard.

That's the good news. The bad news is that the live, and usually longer, interview gives Molly the chance to use *all* of the interview techniques she's learned and practiced.

She'll also have a chance to pass judgment on more than your words and the sound of your voice. She'll be, as the pessimists might put it, watching you squirm.

The Trained Interviewer's Arsenal

Let's take a look at the techniques that Molly will use once you've passed muster over the telephone. Remember, she is trained and practiced in the science of interviewing to a degree that has probably never been even dreamed of by the hiring manager—the person you're hoping to work for (unless of course you're applying for a job in the personnel department). And it is the hiring manager, you know, who will really decide if you'll be walking to work or just walking the pavement next week.

Nevertheless, Molly Ackroyd is the gatekeeper.

You must get past her to get to the less scientific selection interview that will be conducted by your boss-to-be.

Let's start with what is, for most candidates, the worst possible test.

The Stress Interview

Anyone who's been through one of these never forgets it. Becoming increasingly common, the *stress interview* is designed to get past the pleasantries and the veneer and see what the candidate is *really* made of.

I was subjected to a stress interview before I'd ever heard of the technique—not the best way to prepare, believe me—the worst possible scenario for any candidate.

Some years ago, I applied for an editorial position at a major publishing company and made it past the first hurdle, a screening interview conducted in the corporate office.

Next, I was invited to come back to meet the Director of Personnel, Mary Simonoff. Mary greeted me pleasantly and led me back to her rather palatial office. We exchanged a few more pleasantries as I took my seat and settled in.

Before I knew it, I felt as if I were undergoing a police interrogation in a country cited frequently for human rights violations.

Assuming that I had been spoken of highly by the screening interviewer, I was shocked when Mary began questioning my credentials, sarcastically soliciting the reasons I had majored in liberal arts rather than something "practical," and asking me what in the world made me think that I could edit a magazine, even though I had been doing just that for years.

Mary's questions were fired quickly, and each successive question veered dizzyingly to a completely unrelated topic. One question would be about my work experience; the next, about what I did to stay fit; the next, about my favorite movie.

Mary's questions did exactly what I later found they were intended to do—they made me feel confused, fearful, hostile. I behaved badly, answered as many questions as I could in monosyllables, avoided looking Mary in the eye.

Needless to say, I was not offered the job.

I began our discussion of the interviewing process with a description of this technique because it emphasizes some very important lessons about *all* interviews:

- No matter how stressful the situation, stay calm. Never take your eyes from the interviewer. When he or she finishes asking a question, take a few seconds to compose yourself and your answer.

- Recognize the situation for what it is—an artificial scenario designed to see how you react under pressure. The interviewer (probably) has nothing against you personally.

- Don't get despondent. It's easy to think that the interviewer has taken a strong dislike to you and that your chances are nil. That's not the case. The stress interview is designed to see if you will become depressed, hostile and flustered when the going gets tough.

- Watch your tone of voice. It's easy to become sarcastic during a stress interview because, presuming you don't realize what the interviewer is up to, you'll assume he's lost his mind.

Covering All Of The Bases

Much more common nowadays is what has come to be known as the **structured** or **database interview**. Although this might sound complicated or highly technological, both terms refer only to the fact that the interviewer must be careful to ask the same comprehensive set of questions of all candidates.

By asking exactly the same set of questions of every candidate, the theory goes, the interviewer will be able to accurately and fairly compare them. In other words, it allows the hiring organization to establish a complete database on each candidate (the term has nothing to do with computers, although computers might be used to store, retrieve and organize the data gathered) so that eventually it's comparing "apples to apples."

The structured interview can be conducted by more than one person. You will notice interviewers in these situations referring to a long list of questions, checking off things or writing out summaries of your answers.

Because of its comprehensiveness, the structured interview will drain you. You must be prepared to answer questions about your education, related experiences, personal likes and dislikes, interpersonal skills, management skills, if you've had the opportunity to supervise, and just about anything else remotely connected to your skills, personality, experience and "potential."

If you haven't reviewed (or worse, even prepared) your personal inventory sheets prior to *this* type of interview, you will be unable to answer a number of questions *about yourself*—a situation guaranteed to make you look and feel pretty dorky.

The Targeted Interview

A kissing cousin of the structured interview is the *targeted interview.* It is narrower in scope, with nearly all of the questions designed to mine information about the specific skills the employer has deemed necessary for success on the job.

During a targeted interview for a sales position in a remote office, for instance, you might be asked many questions about your interpersonal skills, your self-discipline, the degree to which you procrastinate.

The problem with this type of interview for the candidate is that only a part of the "real you" is given the chance to shine through. You might have several strengths that mitigate a weakness in one area, but the interview might not give you the chance to discuss or demonstrate them.

How To Handle These Scenarios

In either a structured or targeted interview:

- Keep your answers terse, but thorough. You might hope that the interviewer asks you about different parts of your background, but don't talk about areas the interviewer *doesn't* ask about. The interviewer in a structured format wants you to give him the facts...and only the facts that he's asking about.

- Be patient and prepared to answer many questions about just one part of your background or personality. The company has deemed this area an important one for your success.

Let's Suppose Everyone But You Called In Sick And...

Questions like that will tell you that you are in the midst of the increasingly popular *situational interview.*

Like the targeted interview, the situational interview is geared toward measuring the degree to which candidates demonstrate traits deemed key for success in a given position.

The interviewer elicits this information by posing a series of real or hypothetical situations and asking how the candidate would act in each one.

Usually companies are trying to measure candidates' resourcefulness, logic, conceptual thinking ability, creativity, logical thinking. Situational interviews allow candidates to really shine if they:

- Avoid throwing the bull. No type of interview technique invites candidates to be boastful, to exaggerate, or to downright fabricate more than the situational interview. But no other technique exposes that tendency in a candidate so effectively.

  You can admit that a tough situation would make you nervous, might even lead you to momentary panic. Honesty is key when faced with this line of questioning.

  Show that you have a grasp of the real world and that you realize you have a lot to learn about the business. This will be much more effective than trying to act like Lee Iacocca.

- Think about how you'll answer questions when faced with hypothetical scenarios. "You're faced with a production deadline and several people in your department have called in sick..." "Your biggest customer says he's tired of having the company change salesmen on him and he's taking all of his business to a competitor..."

Theory Why

It is not the purpose of this book to frighten you. But forewarned, as they say, is forearmed.

As someone with little or no experience, you represent something of a conundrum for personnel professionals. They are well-schooled in interview theory, and the belief that holds sway in the field is that "Past performance and behavior are the single most reliable factors known in predicting future performance and behavior" (Richard H. Beatty, president of the Bradford Group, an executive search firm).

Given the fact that you have no experience, you don't fit in with the basic theory of interviews. The zealous screening interviewer, therefore, will be trying to ferret out information about your college performance, your personality, your personal interactive style that will be predictive of "future performance."

As a new kid on the block, you are making their job a little more difficult to do well, or to do as scientifically. They might not like that, and might be more tempted to try out hypothetical questions, stress techniques, and other means to get at the real you.

A track record would obviate the need for this type of performance test.

It's Downhill From Here...Sort Of

This might seem awfully complicated. But remember, personnel professionals are usually the only people at a company trained in sophisticated interviewing techniques.

However, the interview with the hiring manager, as we will see in the next chapter, has its own challenges and opportunities for you to demonstrate why you're the best person for the job.

Chapter 5

Here There Be Dragons

The Interview With The Hiring Manager

Right now you're probably thinking, "Hey, I'd be doing really well if I make it past the screening interviewer, who has been trained in this stuff. The hiring manager probably doesn't know as much about interviewing, so getting past him will be a piece of cake."

Wrong!

Skilled interviewers—those conducting the screening interviews—are comfortable and amply experienced in the interview process and are ready with a set of questions that they'll automatically ask unless you turn them off relatively quickly.

They will stay in charge of the interview, not let it meander down some dead-end sidetrack.

And they usually won't ask any questions that they are not legally permitted to ask.

In other words, they know what they're doing, how to do it, and are confident in their skills and knowledge. Consequently, *they're easier to interview with.*

Almost surely, hiring managers will lack some or *all* of the screening interviewers' knowledge, experience and skill of interviewing. They therefore pose a much greater challenge and require *more* preparation on your part.

Flying By The Seat Of Their Pants

Why are hiring managers, for the most part, inferior interviewers? The reason is that very, very few managers in corporate America actually know what it takes to hire the right candidate. Most of them have had *no* formal training in conducting an interview.

What's more, most managers conducting interviews are only slightly less comfortable than the candidates sitting opposite them.

I Got A Feeling

Remember what I said in Chapter 3 about knowledge equalling confidence? Well, hiring managers lack confidence, or possess only false confidence, about their ability to conduct a penetrating, conclusive interview.

Why is the hiring manager's scant knowledge of interviewing potentially dangerous to you? Well, it can mean that he will decide you are not the best candidate because he didn't ask the *right* questions, asked *vague* questions, or asked the *wrong* questions. In other words, he might make a hiring decision based on factors that have *virtually little or nothing to do with you or your actual qualifications!*

Just as the screening interviewer is looking for a set of facts that will help him or her give candidates a pass or fail grade, the hiring manager is looking for insights into the personality of the candidate, into what makes you tick.

He is looking for just enough information to allow his intuition to take over. In other words, facts are *not* his goal in an interview. Instead, he is looking for a candidate he

can *feel good about hiring.* He is not only looking for
measurable skills, but the more subjective sense of "organizational fit."

The things the hiring manager is hoping to get out of
the interview can be elusive. If he is a skilled interviewer,
he will use techniques like the situational interview to get a
sense of how the candidate will perform on the job. If he is
unskilled, as is usually the case, he will be almost passive-
ly hoping that the candidate will do a certain "something"
during the interview that will say to him, "Hey, I'm the one
for you."

Therefore, your goal during the interview with the hiring manager is to inspire his confidence in you. In many
ways, you'll be on your own, in unchartered waters, much
like the early explorers sailing into territory noted on maps
as "Here There Be Dragons."

The hiring manager is more likely to ask open-ended
questions, is more likely to lose control of the interview,
and is more prone to meander.

In this chapter, the most important in the book, I'll
discuss how to inspire the hiring manager's confidence in
you, how to field questions like, "So, tell me about yourself,"
and how to know when it's appropriate for you to seize
control of the interview.

Inspiring Confidence

At one time, I was trying to fill two production positions
at my publishing company after I had decided to install
desktop publishing, a technology that was at that time still
in its infancy.

I was looking for candidates who knew something
about basic book production and could show me they had
the ability and willingness to learn about the new technology.

As a result, my hiring criteria were much more vague than usual. Into this situation walked Eric. He had a small amount of experience in journal publishing, and even less experience using computers for anything at all. But I hired him. What convinced me to hire him was his enthusiasm.

He was so interested in learning desktop publishing that he couldn't stop asking questions about it. He'd read a good deal about it, could talk about its intricacies for hours and even pointedly informed me he wished they had taught it at school.

Despite only one year's working experience, Eric exhibited a great deal of confidence and demonstrated that he was not only excited to learn about the new technology, but convinced that he could.

Hiring Eric paid off, despite his seeming lack of all the right experience. He took to desktop like the proverbial fish to water, learning it with such rapidity that within one year I put him in charge of coordinating repairs, buying equipment and evaluating new software packages.

The lesson for *you* in this story is that confidence and enthusiasm are probably the two key things that a hiring manager is looking for. I think that even if Eric had had *no* experience in production, I'd have hired him because he demonstrated such an overwhelming willingness to learn and work hard.

Putting Out The Right Vibes

How can you convey your confidence and enthusiasm to a hiring manager? Here are some tips:

- *Think of the interview as an adventure* and try to enjoy it. I know that might sound strange, but you *can* make even the toughest interview an enjoyable experience if you display enthusiasm and get the hiring manager interested in you.

One friend of mine, who was considering going to law school, took the LSATs while he was making up his mind. He scored pretty badly, so he signed up to take them again. By the time the next test date rolled around, he'd decided to pursue another career option.

He went ahead and took the LSATs again anyway, thinking of them as an experience, an adventure. Besides, he wanted to see how well he could do. He scored 200 points higher. He certainly hadn't prepared more. But his attitude for taking the test was right. *He felt no pressure,* which allowed his mind to perform at its best.

- *Be enthusiastic* about the position, about your accomplishments, about what you've found out about the company. I remember one candidate who sat like a bump on a log throughout an interview for a junior editorial position, asked no questions, and gave the tersest replies to mine. I cut the interview short because I felt she didn't want the job. I was shocked when she repeatedly called to see if I'd made my final choice. In fact, she *desperately* wanted the position; she just had not conveyed that enthusiasm to me when it really *counted.*

- *Be honest.* Express enthusiasm only about the things you are truly enthusiastic about. Phoniness will not sell the hiring manager on you.

- *Be polite.* You're not expected to sit with your hands crossed primly in your lap, but remember to be tactful during the interview. For instance, if the interviewer says something offensive to you, don't jump down his or her throat. Just pause a moment and say something like, "Well, I know many people feel that way, but I think ..." In other words, be a diplomat.

- *Keep on smiling.* Sure, you're accustomed to giving people a big smile when you shake hands with them. In the interview, keep on smiling. A smile makes you appear agreeable and pleasant. And who wouldn't want to work with a pleasant and agreeable person like you?

- *Make lots of eye contact.* Have you ever known someone who wouldn't look you in the eye? You begin to wonder what that person has to hide. Make eye contact while you're shaking hands with the interviewer and periodically throughout the interview.

    Don't stare or make continuous eye contact— that would make anyone feel uncomfortable.

- *Be positive.* It's best to keep negative words out of your interview vocabulary to the extent possible. Let's say you switched majors and the interviewer asks why. Don't say, "I couldn't stand the professors in the economics department; I just had to get out of there." Instead, try something like, "I got a lot out of studying economics, but I became absolutely fascinated with marketing, so I decided to make the switch."

    Repeat to yourself one thousand times "Be positive!" before you go on any interview. In rehearsing your answers to interview questions, take all of the negative words out.

"So, Tell Me A Little About Yourself"

This is the favorite question of the trained interviewer, because it gives him or her the opportunity to study a host of reactions from verbal cues to body language.

But it is also the favorite of the *untrained* interviewer for quite a different reason—simply because he or she usually doesn't know what else to ask.

It's therefore a good idea to assume that this question will be put to you and to prepare for it the way presidential candidates prepare for televised debates—by developing and rehearsing a set reply. Otherwise, you may be fated to react like the narrator in essayist J. B. Priestly's piece, "All About Ourselves:"

> "Now tell me," said the lady, "all about yourself." The effect was instantaneous, shattering. Up to that moment, I had been feeling expansive; I was self-confident, alert, ready to give a good account of myself in the skirmish of talk. If I had been asked my opinion of anything between here and Sirius, I would have given it at length, and I was quite prepared to talk of places I had never seen and books I had never read; I was ready to lie, and to lie boldly and well. Had she not made that *fatal* demand, I would have roared...(emphasis added).

When *you* are asked that "fatal" question, remember the first cardinal rule of interviewing: The hiring manager wants to feel good about you. Your primary goal is to let him or her do just that.

And the second cardinal rule: The hiring manager wants you to make him feel confident that hiring you will be a good decision. Your answer to this question should be targeted to doing just that.

Taking Stock Once Again

To prepare an excellent answer to this question, look back at the personal inventory I urged you to prepare in

Chapter 3. Most important in preparing your answer are items you listed under the headings:

- Strongest skills.
- Greatest areas of knowledge.
- Strongest parts of my personality.
- The things I do best.
- Key accomplishments.

Take that information and turn it into a speech of about 250 words (less than one minute). Here is a proposed outline of this brief verbal picture of YOU:

1. Key accomplishments.
2. Key strengths demonstrated by those accomplishments.
3. The importance of these accomplishments and strengths for the hiring manager.

Here's an example of a solid one-minute speech:

I fell in love with engineering in high school and have wanted to work in aerospace ever since. My internship at ABC Aircraft gave me a tremendous amount of experience on the drafting table and in the use of computer-aided engineering. ABC called me back for two subsequent summer internships.

I was a straight-A student in my major field of study, physics, and have a paper being considered for publication in the Journal of Metal Fatigue, something, I'm told, that not many undergraduates have accomplished.

Of course, I learned a great deal in college, but I think the greatest learning experience was at ABC. I realized the importance of being a self-starter, how to take initiative when I had ideas, and how to get along with engineers with far more experience and knowledge than I.

I'm tremendously excited about the prospect of working at your company. I have long admired its Airloft jet engine and the fact that you are continually at the forefront of the industry. I've also read a great deal about your computer-aided engineering and manufacturing systems and am excited about learning more about this technology.

Also, your policy of encouraging scientists and engineers to publish and win recognition in their fields fits in perfectly with my professional goals. While I think that working for a firm can be extremely rewarding, the greatest achievement for a scientist is the recognition of his peers.

Can you tell me, Mr. Smith, how the installation of CAD/CAM has improved the effectiveness of your department?

In this little speech, the interviewee has:

1. Bragged a bit about his grades and the area of his knowledge (metal fatigue) without getting carried away.

2. Shown that he knows the difference between college and the "real world" and recognizes the value of his experience in the latter.

3. Demonstrated a knowledge of the company's products and personnel policies.

4. Expressed enthusiasm for working at the company.

5. Talked about some of his personal strengths (the tendency to be a self starter, ambitious, the ability to learn new things quickly).

6. Taken temporary control of the interview at the end of his answer by asking Mr. Smith an informed question.

Not bad for a couple of hundred words! Write your little speech on a piece of paper, rewrite it, rewrite it...then rewrite it. You want it to sound natural and conversational but to include all the key points you want to emphasize.

It should not have a lot of dependant clauses and tricky constructions, because people don't talk that way unless they've memorized a speech, and you *don't* want to sound like Bob Hope reading from some internal cue cards. That would certainly give the interviewer a bad impression. But if you have a speech like the one above, you'll knock him out.

Also, anticipate the questions the interviewer might ask *after* you give your speech about yourself and prepare answers for *those* questions. You certainly don't want to look as if you have nothing more to say after you've finished your canned presentation.

Taking Control Of The Interview

Those going to interview for their first jobs—and even candidates with many years of experience for several different companies—go into the interview thinking they are there for only one reason: to answer questions.

Nothing could be further from the truth. Yes, you are going to the interview for only one reason, but that reason is *to sell the interviewer on the fact that you are the best person for the job.*

You will do this by *giving* terrific answers to the interviewer's questions, by *asking* great questions about the company and the position, and by *telling* the interviewer the things about yourself that you want him to know.

Let's say you went to an automobile showroom knowing just a little about a particular car. You are approached by an affable salesman who answers your questions but doesn't volunteer any information you hadn't asked about and asks no questions of you. Do you think you'd end up buying a car from him?

Most candidates approach the job interview like this hapless salesman. They are prepared to answer questions, but hesitate to volunteer information unless it's asked for— even if that information concerns some of their key talents or strengths.

Dmn't miss the opportunity the interview gives you to sell yourself. The fact that a customer walked into the showroom should have been enough to inspire that car salesman to do his best. Similarly, the fact that you've been called in for the interview has given you a chance to sell yourself. Don't blow it just because the interviewer doesn't ask the questions you were hoping he would. Find some means to give your answers anyway.

Standing Out In The Crowd

At one company I worked for, a manager, who I'll call Howard, ran a large and growing department and, consequently, did a great deal of hiring.

The personnel department began to notice that he had the highest ratio of candidates interviewed to candidates hired of any manager at the company, and that many of the candidates that he turned down seemed absolutely terrific to everybody else.

Finally, the director of personnel asked one successful candidate what the interview with Howard had been like. The candidate said, "Well, it wasn't what I expected. He just talked to me about the company and the position for about 30 minutes and then asked me if I had any questions. I think I was lucky that I had a lot of good questions."

From that time on, the director of personnel would tell those she considered leading candidates to "ask a lot of good questions during your interview with Howard."

The reason Howard employed his rather stilted interview technique was that he was a shy, introverted man who happened to excel at certain important areas of his job, though interviewing certainly wasn't one of them.

Howard felt in complete command while talking about the company, but had a great deal of trouble making even the smallest bit of small talk.

Therefore, only candidates who found some way to differentiate themselves, who took some initiative, would stand out in Howard's mind after the dozen or so interviews he might conduct to fill each opening.

Seize The Day

Like Howard, many less-experienced interviewers often have a tendency to run on at the mouth. In those situations, you must take charge—ask questions constantly.

If the interviewer has been speaking non-stop for ten minutes when he says, "We've increased sales 20 percent every year for the past decade," politely interrupt with a question like, "How has the company maintained such growth? That's very impressive in a mature industry like the bowling-pin spotting equipment market."

Talking Faster Doesn't Help

At the opposite extreme is the interviewer who will let the poor candidate talk and talk in answer to a single question because he has so few others to ask.

If you're faced with such a situation, be careful and watch how the interviewer is reacting to your soliloquy. If he exhibits what seems to be a negative response—crossing his arms across his chest, sitting bolt upright in his chair, fidgeting, tapping his fingers on the desk, shuffling papers—change the subject or ask him a question. You're not getting anywhere by continuing to flap your gums.

Don't make the mistake of noting his discomfort, getting nervous, and talking *faster* because you think that might help you get around to whatever the interviewer really wants to hear. He might just want to hear his own voice, not yours, for a minute or two!

I'll discuss interview behavior at greater length in Chapter 7. For now, just remember that the interview with the hiring manager is apt to be quite different from that with the personnel department.

Because the hiring manager is less experienced, the interview is probably going to present more of a challenge, but if you handle it correctly, it also presents a greater opportunity to allow your key strengths to shine through.

I again urge you to be prepared with a little speech about who you are and to be ready to answer a far greater number of open-ended questions (who, what, where, when, why, how).

If you want to use your school experiences as a reference, think of the personnel department interviews as the multiple-choice and true-or-false parts of an exam, while the hiring manager's interview is more like the essay section.

You have to know the facts for both, but the second requires you to explain the implications of those facts.

Also remember, that, unlike the screening interviewer, the hiring manager's primary goal on an interview is not a set of facts, but a feeling. He wants to feel confident that you are the best person for the job. Don't let a lack of preparedness or a hesitancy to use this opportunity for your benefit keep you from a job you want and deserve.

Chapter 6

Walk Right In, Sit Right Down

You Don't Get A Second
Chance At First Impressions

If there's one notion that all interviewers share, it's that candidates are hitting them with their best shot. They are convinced that what they see and hear during the interview—how you dress, the degree of politeness you exhibit, your grooming, your articulateness, your social skills, etc.—are the best you've got.

After all, you're trying to convince total strangers that they should invest substantial amounts of time and money in you. Why *wouldn't* you look and act your best?

Now I'm sure some of you *think* you look best in a Hawaiian shirt and cutoffs. And you might be right. But the interview is one time in your life when it's probably best to put aside individuality in choice of wardrobe.

This is the one chapter in which I can tyrannically say that there *is* only *one* right way to do things. In discussing how you should dress for an interview, I feel entirely comfortable throwing impartiality and individualism out the window. You will be playing the interviewer's game. If you want the job, you must play by his or her rules.

How Men Should Dress
For The Interview

There is no magic or imagination required to pick out the best outfit a man should wear on a job interview—just make like Betsy Ross and think red, white, and blue. Red tie, white shirt, blue suit.

Invest now in a navy blue wool, wool worsted, or wool-blend suit. It will look better and last longer than other materials, and it will go with almost anything. Select a three-piece or single-breasted two-piece fashion, preferably vented.

This might sound awfully old-fashioned, but for most jobs, the best bet is to dress conservatively, with minimal flash.

The shirt should be long-sleeved, professionally starched and pressed (it's well-worth the buck or two), and have no fraying at the collar or cuffs. Button-down Oxford or spread collars are best.

The tie should be a silk foulard in a subdued red with a stripe or small pattern in the same blue as your suit. This will add a bit of safe sexiness to your ensemble.

Remember that you should not wear any pins, cuff-links, or ties that bear a religious or service affiliation. Why risk turning an interviewer off unless you want to make your outside affiliation a basis for your employment?

(A possible exception might arise if you discover through your research that your interviewer and you share a common affiliation. In such a case, for example, wearing a subtle Masonic pin might well work positively on an interviewer who's a Mason. The danger, even in this case, is that you will so impress the interviewer that he or she will bring you around to meet some other people who *don't* share that affiliation. Better, in general, to avoid the outer display and, if you've discovered something in common, simply work it into your conversation in a diplomatic and natural way.)

Your watch should not be a Swatch or other stylish plastic make, but a conservative model with a stretch or leather band—it needn't be expensive.

Wear black or navy blue socks that cover your entire calf. If you cross your legs during the interview, you don't want any of your rugby injuries to show.

And don't forget to polish your shoes—black, conservative loafers or lace-ups with a low heel.

How Women Should Dress For The Interview

As you'll notice throughout your career, women have a great deal more flexibility than men in their choice of business attire. However, the greater number of options doesn't imply complete freedom in the interview situation.

Women must take care to avoid what could be considered provocative clothing—V-necks, short hemlines, patterned stockings. They should wear dresses or suits in muted colors and non-shiny fabrics, such as wool. Women should also avoid large fashion jewelry, oversized handbags, open-toed shoes, and too-high heels. You'll want to look much more like Sigourney Weaver than early-Melanie Griffith in the film "Working Girl."

Unisex Grooming For Success

There are several grooming rules that apply to both sexes:

- Don't go to the interview too heavily scented. It's not that you shouldn't wear perfume or cologne, but don't wear so much that memories of you will linger in the room for the rest of the week.

- Bring along a brief or attache case, either black or brown.

- Pay particular attention on the morning of your interview to hygiene and grooming. Hair, including mustaches and beards, should be neatly trimmed. Avoid excessive hairspray and, if possible, the types of hairstyles that would require it. Make sure that your fingernails are cleaned and clipped. And don't have any spicy foods on the way to the appointment.

Body Language

You'll have so much to think about during the interview that you might very well overlook what your body is up to. I watched a candidate pick at a mole during an entire 45-minute interview, oblivious to how uncomfortable this might make even the most stout-hearted (and strong-stomached) interviewer, of which I was not one. Here are some tips that will keep your body from betraying you.

Leave Some Fingers Intact

When you get to the reception area, take off your coat and hat and hang them in a closet if one is available. This will ensure that you have one less thing to fumble with later on. If you are in the reception area for a while, keep your hands exposed, not in your pockets. This will help dry them so that they are not too clammy.

When the interviewer comes to meet you, extend your hand, look him straight in the eye, and say, "Pleased to meet you, Mr. Eggman. I am Dee Walrus." Make sure that your handshake is firm, but not crushing, and don't worry about your palms being a little damp. This is not an easy moment for any candidate.

Follow the interviewer into his office. This is a good time to make some small talk. "My, these offices are beautiful! How long have you been at this address?" Or, "We're lucky to have such cool weather in August (or such warm weather in November)."

Remember, try to keep your conversation positive. It's a bad idea to start off with something like, "Boy, I can't stand this muggy weather," or, "I thought I would never find this place." You'll cause the interviewer to think, at least on a subconscious level, that you're a negative person or that you secretly wish you were somewhere else.

Sitting Pretty

As you enter the interviewer's office, wait for his cue as to where you should sit if there is more than one obvious choice. If offered any chair, choose the one closest to and opposite the interviewer's chair. This will help demonstrate your confidence.

Don't immediately begin rooting around in your briefcase for your resume. Make a little bit more small talk to help you—and the interviewer—ease into the Q & A.

Again, the conversational icebreaker should be fairly innocuous, but upbeat. "How many employees do you have here at headquarters?" "This part of the state sure has seen a lot of development recently, hasn't it?"

If you are seated at a table, interlock your fingers and keep your hands on the tabletop. This will keep you from fidgeting.

If seated on a chair or couch unprotected, keep your feet flat on the floor (don't cross your legs), interlock your fingers and keep your hands in your lap.

This is not to say that you shouldn't talk with your hands. If you're like me and do so quite naturally, be yourself. But when you're not using your hands to make a point, keep them folded and still.

Make eye contact throughout the entire interview, but don't overdo it. You're not engaged in a staring contest with Clint Eastwood. And staring without pause at the interviewer will *not* make his day.

Keep an eye on your body—figuratively, that is. Be sure that you don't slouch, which may convey an impression of laziness or sloppiness. On the other hand, don't sit there like a Marine at attention. It will make you seem edgy, overly aggressive, a real "Type A" personality.

Are We Nervous?

If you have a pulse, of course you are! The interview is a difficult situation, but you can't allow nervousness to make you freeze at the wheel. Here are some tips on relaxing so that you'll be at your best during the interview:

- Arrive in plenty of time. Get to the vicinity of the building, if possible, a good twenty minutes before your appointment and to the reception area at least ten minutes early. The fear of being late for a very important date can put you in a state of high anxiety.

- Ask the receptionist for a key to the restroom before she announces you. This will allow you time to comb your hair, straighten your clothing, wash and dry your hands. This pit stop serves a dual purpose: You'll be sure you look your best and, by concentrating on details, you'll take your mind off the scary unknown—at least momentarily.

- While you're waiting for the interviewer to greet you, take some deep, deep breaths. This will help stem the "fight-or-flight" response that all of us experience when anxious. Deep breathing helps even the worst phobics control their fears. It's an effective way to overcome the physiological causes of panic.

- Again, concentrate on minutiae. Check to see that your resume is readily available in your briefcase. Pick up a magazine and read the most meaningless article you can find. But avoid newspapers, since the newsprint probably will come off on your sweaty palms.

- Remember that the interviewer is not the only one with something to learn. You have come to the interview to find out about the company. *You* will be in charge of some parts of the interview—you are not merely some specimen on a slide to be studied for the next hour. Think of yourself as an important part of the interview, not just one of many interchangeable candidates.

- Think of the interview as an adventure, as a learning experience, as a chance to brag about yourself and actually (or hopefully) get rewarded for it.

Don't Get Off To A Bad Start

All of the advice is fairly easy to remember. Your choice of wardrobe is limited. And you have to remember to be enthusiastic, polite, and calm.

However, *following* the advice can be a bit more difficult when your heart is beating like mad as you head to the interviewer's office.

Practice deep breathing—that's right, practice it—so that it comes easily and automatically when stress begins to set in.

And have one of your friends or relatives play the role of the Grand Inquisitor so you can rehearse how you will act during the interview.

If you have access to the equipment, videotape a role-play interview. You'll notice little tics and habits that you might be able to control so they don't distract the interviewer from the YOU underneath that nice blue suit.

Chapter 7

In The Spotlight

The Finer Points Of Interviewee Technique

Read this chapter for extra credit.

Until now, I've discussed in broad strokes how you should conduct yourself during the interview. In this chapter, I'll present some of the finer points that will help you "score big" when you meet with the personnel department or the hiring manager.

I know that it seems as if you already have a lot to think about for these one-hour (or, more likely, less) exercises. But some of the lessons in this chapter will really help you stand out from the madding crowd of candidates.

Demonstrate An Interest In The Interviewer

Surprisingly enough, interviewers *are* human (for the most part). Like you, they respond positively to those who demonstrate a genuine interest in them. And they become impatient or bored with those who seem too self-absorbed.

Therefore, you can score big points if you demonstrate an interest in the interviewer. This is particularly true if the interview is with the hiring manager. After all, he is looking for an individual whose mission will be to help him, someone who will be attentive and responsive. Showing an interest in the interviewer will go a long way toward convincing him that you will care about *his* needs and goals after you begin working for him.

Out On A Limb

A friend of mine landed a prime position at a brand-new company launched by a legendary entrepreneur in his industry. He was selected over many good candidates for this plum position. This was a triumph for my friend, especially since this entrepreneur, who I'll call Larry, was known to be difficult to impress.

My friend, Cameron, told this story about the interview:

> *Here was Larry, a multi-millionaire, sitting with a secretary and one other employee in this nearly empty 10,000 square feet of office shell. They had lights, a phone, a postage machine, some furniture, and that's about it. There were workmen off in one corner building some walls for his office.*
>
> *Naturally, I was expecting a little more, and somehow these strange circumstances completely wiped away my nervousness. When Larry stood up to greet me, I introduced myself, then said, "I bet it has been a long time since you opened your own mail."*
>
> *At first, I couldn't believe I had done that, but Larry laughed and off we went.*

For the next hour, Cameron "had a ball" talking with Larry about the launch of what promised to be an exciting company. He stayed loose during the entire interview, real-izing that his going out on a limb had paid off. He felt—and expressed—enthusiasm for the utter lack of structure at the new company and "Larry really picked up on that. I could sense his violent dislike for big structures, so I took pains to stress *my* preference for lean, mean companies."

Cameron's move was risky, but it worked because it displayed confidence, it implied a knowledge of Larry's background, and it suggested that Cameron was well aware that Larry wanted this company to grow to the point that a mailroom would make sense.

Controlling Interest

Cameron had a great deal of control in the interview because he continued to demonstrate an interest in Larry's problems. In fact, to almost any of the challenges Larry discussed, Cameron would ask, "How did that work?" or, "At ABC, we had a similar problem. Let me tell you briefly what worked."

Cameron came across as an interested, sympathetic problem solver. He got an offer for the job that afternoon.

Granted, Cameron was presented with a golden inter-view opportunity. But he had the experience and *chutzpah* to seize upon it and play it to the hilt.

Oh, Sure You Can!

You're probably saying, "But I can't do anything like that."

Maybe not. It's not often that opportunities like the one Cameron had come along. What's more, you don't have the type of job experience you can draw on to "wow" an inter-viewer.

But you *can* display your interest in the interviewer with the simplest of comments: "I recognized you from your picture in the employee newsletter. Congratulations on your recent promotion." "Is that a Macintosh SE on your desk? I've heard great things about those machines. How do you like it?" "That's a wonderful photograph on your wall. Where was it taken?"

Don't overdo this. Nothing is worse than "smarminess," unless the interviewer is an egomaniac.

Build A Vocabulary Of Positive Action Words

What! A vocabulary lesson for a 45-minute interview?

Granted, this might seem like overkill, but you'll use this vocabulary on your resume, in your job-hunting letters, during the interview, in your follow-up letters...and in every business letter you'll write for the rest of your life.

Here it is. Read it over every day. Build some of it into the little speech about yourself discussed in Chapter 5.

Ability	Enthusiasm	Managed
Achieved	Established	Monitored
Accelerated	Evaluated	Motivated
Accurate	Excelled	Organized
Analyzed	Focus	Planned
Capable	Generated	Prepared
Conceived	Guided	Presented
Conceptualized	Initiated	Pride
Determined	Implemented	Proficiency
Developed	Introduced	Programmed
Directed	Improved	Promoted
Effective	Launched	Recommended
Energy	Lead	Revised

Reorganized	Supervised	Updated
Responsible	Systematic	Urgency
Streamlined	Tested	Utilized
Strengthened	Thorough	Vital
Solved	Trained	

This is just a sample, but you get the idea. Always think in terms of positive, action words. They needn't be "five-dollar" words, but they should be words that stand out from normal conversational lingo.

Concentrate, Concentrate, Then Concentrate

Have you ever been in a conversation and realized that while you've been speaking, the person supposedly listening to you was thinking only about what *he'd* say next? You'd probably think that person was pretty self-centered and obviously uninterested in you and what you had to say.

Employers go one step further. They think that people demonstrating such behavior during a job interview are lacking one of the most important skills a good employee needs: the ability to listen, to be attentive, to react to the situation.

During an interview, many candidates have a tendency to let their guard down after a certain amount of time. Oh, they start off enthusiastically and attentively, full of vim and vigor, but once they think they've gotten through the toughest part of the interview, they start to relax .

Don't do it. Don't get *too* relaxed. You should be concentrating on everything the interviewer says and asks so that you can formulate impressive questions and tell him precisely what he wants to know.

I recommend that unless you have an adverse reaction to caffeine, have a cup or two of coffee or tea about thirty minutes before the interview so that your mind is hopping Just don't overdo it—a fidgity caffeine overdose is hell to deal with during an interview!

Answer The Question

After you give an answer, look your interviewer in the eye and prepare to listen, and I mean *listen,* to the next question. Then give him what he wants.

If he's asked for a specific set of facts, don't lose yourself in a mountain of details and give him all of the implications and explanations he *didn't* ask for.

Terseness and directness will score big points for you. Long-windedness will make the interviewer wish you'd leave and go bend some other manager's ear.

Now, Wait A Second

Many interviewees seem to be under the false assumption that they will score extra points on their interviews if they answer questions quickly. They begin speaking as soon as the interviewer finishes with the question, usually rushing headlong into an answer they soon wish they could revise, or worse yet, withdraw entirely!

It's a much better idea to allow for a short pause after the question so that you can compose a terrific answer.

Short pause not enough? Then stall for more time with phrases like "Now, let me see," "I'm glad you asked that question." Or paraphrase the question and repeat it back to the interviewer. The latter choice would go something like this:

Interviewer: Tell me, what made you decide to change your major six times during your undergraduate days?

Candidate (after a short pause): Why did I change my major so often? Well, let me see, there were several reasons while I was an underclassman, but..." Without a lot of "umms" and "uhhs", the candidate has fairly successfully stalled for time.

(Hey, it worked for Ronald Reagan, didn't it?)

No Question Is A Throwaway

Some questions might seem unimportant, but don't ever *treat* them that way. Give equally careful consideration to every answer.

For instance, one acquaintance of mine thought that enthusiasm and a good work ethic should weigh more heavily in his consideration of candidates for most positions than their experience or education.

So many of the seemingly innocent questions he asked were designed to evaluate to what degree candidates possessed these characteristics. He asked about hobbies, believing that those without interests were either dull or lazy.

He'd also give careful consideration to candidates' comments about the weather, getting to the interview, the hectic days after college.

Candidates who consistently expressed negative views or started whining about these matters were not considered for hire.

So, be on your guard—remember that most employers are looking for enthusiasm, confidence, dependability, and vigor.

If you whine your way through questions about the weather, you won't be thought of as someone possessing energy and the right attitude.

And if you point out that it took you hours to find the interviewer's office because you failed to get detailed enough directions, well, so much for your competence and dependability.

Be Decisive

Open-ended questions are a double-edged sword. In Chapter 6, I urged you to prepare a little speech to deliver when you're asked, "How would you describe yourself?"

Well, there are a lot of other open-ended questions likely to come up—"What are your key strengths?" "What are your goals?" "What accomplishment are you proudest of?" "Why did you choose your major?" "Why do you want to re-locate to our area?" "What would your best friend say about you?"

You should have prepared the answers to many of these kinds of questions. Whether or not you remember them in the interview room, be decisive in your answers.

Avoid the kinds of answers too many candidates give to these types of questions: "Boy, that's a tough one. Hmmm, I've never thought about that, but I guess if I had to choose one accomplishment, I would have to say that it might be making the Dean's list seven straight semesters. Although I'm really proud of my Eagle Scout pin. No, I'd have to say the Dean's List. Definitely. ...and the Eagle Scout pin."

Such answers make candidates look incredibly indeci-sive—not exactly a trait employers are looking for. So, after pausing to consider your answer and stalling smoothly, hit the interviewer with your best shot—and stick with it.

So *don't* add, "Well, gee, maybe neither was really the one I'm proudest of. Maybe it's the fact that I earned a lot of my college expenses during my summers." Sure, you want to score that point, but wait for another opportunity.

The Sounds Of Silence

Nothing is worse for a stand-up comic than silence, hence, the old line, "I know you're out there. I can hear you breathing," from the comedian desperate for a laugh.

If you hear the sounds of silence during your interview, you'll probably feel even more desperate. And that's just how some interviewers want you to feel. The most experienced inquisitors use silence to see how a candidate will squirm. And squirm they usually do!

A candidate confronted by interviewer silence will: begin retracting what he just said, restate what he just said in slightly different words, begin volunteering more information than he should. Not helpful reactions.

Avoid doing any of these things. My best advice is the same given to every neophyte sales representative: "Once you've made the sale, shut up." (Granted, it's the lesson that takes most salespeople a lifetime to learn.)

Retracting, restating, muttering, or launching into a complete history of your life when you're faced with interviewer silence will not help your image at all. It will make you appear indecisive.

Or, worse, it might lead you to say things you'd decided you wouldn't say during the interview—the less than rational reasons you switched majors, the fact that you hated your internships, or the fact that you were rejected by seven graduate schools.

When you are finished answering a question, *show* you are done—meet the interviewer's silence with some confident silence of your own. Then, break it with a question so that, once again, you can feel in control of the interview.

Don't Worry, Be Positive

Go into the interview thinking, "I am going to get this job." You'll perform much better if you are confident (but not cocky).

Barry, a business associate of mine, switched jobs five times in the first 15 years of his career. He had very few interviews during those years, but he made the ones he did have really count.

One time, Barry got a call from an executive recruiter (or "headhunter," as they are more commonly known) who wanted to tell him about a terrific new position. When the headhunter got done describing the job, Barry said, "Boy, that job has my name on it. What are they offering?"

The recruiter told Barry the top salary. It wasn't bad, but it was $10,000 less than Barry wanted if he were going to uproot himself again. "Well, Jane," he told the recruiter. "I wanted a lot more money than that."

"That's all I can squeeze out of them," said Jane. "That is the absolute top of the salary range for this position."

Barry was not deterred. "Send me over there," he said. "Once they meet me, they'll come up with the extra dough."

After a great deal of hemming and hawing, Jane gave in. Barry, an experienced and confident interviewer, got the salary he wanted.

Do You Want That Job?

If *you* want the job, go into the interview with the attitude that it's yours for the taking. Don't be cocky, but be confident. Express your enthusiasm for the job, for the opportunity to be considered for it. And be positive about everything, even the weather.

Think of the type of people you would like to work with. They are happy to be on the job, bright, willing to help. Your goal is to convince the interviewer that he'd like to work with *you*.

Do You Know What They're Writing About

Not to make you more nervous, but if you're just graduating from college, you have something else to contend with—your generation has been getting a bad rap in the media. Countless articles in personnel journals and major consumer publications such as *Working Woman* and *Business Week* have characterized you and your peers as a hard-to-manage lot. You're supposedly part of the "the brash pack"—a group of spoiled brats who want the corner office and all the other perks of seniority without being ready to pay the dues everyone else has paid, without even wanting to take the time to learn to do your jobs right.

Sound as if you have a strike against you before you even apply for the job?

With some personnel departments and hiring managers, you do. The fact that you are faced with this disadvantage means that you must try even harder to convince the interviewer that you will be a trainable, hard-working employee...who will wait at least a year before requesting a corner office and a company Mercedes.

And that all those *other* entry-level candidates are the ones the magazines have been writing about!

Chapter 8

And The Survey Says!

The 66 Favorite Interview Questions Of All Time

This is not exactly the most thrilling of hit parades, but it probably will be more useful to you than any of Dick Clark's.

Like television plots, all interview questions fall into roughly three groups:

1. Factual questions about your job experience and education.

2. Questions designed to determine who you really are, what you're made of.

3. Questions that will help the interviewer predict how you might perform on the job.

In the preceding chapters, I've discussed in a general way how you will answer these questions. This chapter will present a laundry list of questions. There will be a brief discussion about how you should frame your replies after groups of related questions.

You should not spend time preparing answers to all of these questions in advance, writing them down and memorizing them. If you did that, you might not go on your first interview until you were eligible for Medicare. But you should have the necessary facts to answer them in some relatively retrievable portion of your brain.

Questions About What You've Accomplished

1. What extracurricular activities were you active in? What made you choose those? Which of them did you most enjoy? Why?

2. What courses did you like best at college? Which of them did you like the least? Why? What were the factors influencing your choice of major and minor?

3. What did you learn from (or why don't I see any) internships on your resume? How did you get those internships? What was the most valuable thing you learned from each?

4. If you were to start college over again tomorrow, what courses would you take? Why?

5. In what courses did you get your best grades? Why?

6. In what courses did you get your worst grades? Why? How do you think that will affect your performance on the job?

7. What were the factors that led you to select your college?

8. What led you to choose that major over others?

9. What type of student were you?

10. What sort of grades did you get? In your major? In your minor?

11. Which courses did you like the most? Why?

12. Which courses did you like the least? Why?

13 Why did you (or didn't you) decide to go to graduate school?

What The Interviewer Really Wants To Know

These questions might seem prosaic enough, but they all have a hidden agenda. The interviewer is really probing to determine how ambitious and how "trainable" you are.

No company really believes that someone is going to come out of college or graduate school and be immediately productive. Many are willing to invest more and more in training to have people "forget what they learned in school and do things the right way," even if that takes months.

Therefore, the interviewer could very well be probing to see whether you're a know-it-all or sensible enough to know he or she still has a lot to learn.

The interviewer also is probing for the amount of ambition you have and to what extent you are a pampered person used to having his or her own way with little effort.

So, let's say you haven't run up a huge list of extracurricular accomplishments because you really had to hit the books to get good grades. If the interviewer asks, "Why didn't you get more involved in outside activities?" don't reply, "Oh, I spent a lot of time studying and I didn't want those things to get in the way of my social life." Instead, say, "I got involved in a few things. I wish I had done more, but I really was interested in my studies. I cracked the books every night, and that's what enabled me to finish second in the class."

On Question 4, it's a good idea to be decisive, to say that you are convinced you chose the right field, even though it might have taken you a while to find it. "I'm really glad I majored in Pseudoscience. I only wish that I had known a little more about it when I began my studies. I could have taken a couple of other courses in the discipline as an undergraduate."

Questions For Getting To Know You

14. Please tell me a little bit about yourself.

15 What do you consider your key strengths?

16. What do you consider your key weaknesses? What do you think you will do about them?

17. Have you ever had a weakness in the past that you've been able to overcome? How did you accomplish this?

18. Do you think that you'll prefer to work with others or by yourself? Are there experiences you have had in school or in part-time jobs that support that?

19. Do you have any plans to further your education?

20. During your internships (or part-time jobs), what sort of evaluations did you get from supervisors?

21. What supervisor did you like the best? Why did you like him or her?

22. What supervisor did you like the least? What did you not like about him or her?

23. Looking back on the experience, do you think you could have done anything differently to get along with the supervisor a little better?

24. What are some of the things you do in your spare time? What are your favorite hobbies? Do you play any sports?

25. How do you handle yourself when you're having a conflict with someone? Are you confrontational? Do you avoid that person? Why? How do you think you'll behave when you have a problem with a co-worker?

26. If you could change one thing about your personality with a snap of your fingers, what would it be? Why?

27. If I met some of your peers from college, what do you think they would say about you?

Tough, Aren't They?

If you're hit with a series of questions from the list immediately above, you'll feel like you've been put through the wringer.

Only the most annoying people *don't* find it difficult to talk about themselves in a flattering way. And that's what you'll be doing on the interview—constantly blowing your own horn until even you will want to change the tune.

You'll be saying what a great guy your friends think you are, what a pleasure your supervisors thought it was to have you on their team, that there are only a few little adjustments you'd like to make to your personality. Why, this can all sound pretty sickening.

But don't get carried away with yourself. When you're answering these questions:

- Remember that companies are looking for these traits: enthusiasm, confidence, energy, dependability, honesty, pride in work.

- Formulate your answers that suggest these characteristics. Think about what you would want in an ideal employee if *you* owned a company. You'd want problem-solvers, team players, people willing to work hard, people who enjoyed what they were doing, wouldn't you? So do the interviewers you'll be meeting.

A friend of mine had to work his way through college, holding down a number of menial positions totally unrelated to the career he hoped eventually to enter. He simply could not afford to be on low-paying internships during his summers or involve himself in a lot of extracurricular activities. He had to pump gas.

This presented a quandary during his interview at a publishing company, a very internship-oriented field.

He knew questions about these things would come up from his Ivy League interviewer. Therefore, he was prepared with answers like, "I wish I'd had more time to do things like work on the school paper, but whenever I wasn't studying, I pretty much had to work to pay for college. During all of those jobs, though, I learned a number of things that people learn only after they've been in their careers for a while, like how to work with others and how to manage my time."

He thus turned a possible negative into a salient positive.

This list of questions also should emphasize the importance of the Personal Inventory we discussed in Chapter 3. Don't go on your first interview without having written one.

- Remember not to volunteer any negative information about yourself unless you are specifically asked for it. When you *are* asked for it, try to turn it into a positive.

For instance, your answers to Questions 9 and 19 might be: "Well, I have had a problem with procrastination, but I have really solved it. What I learned in college was to work on the tasks I least like first, and then the rest of my assignments seemed easy."

- On questions about self-improvement and future plans, remember that you must exhibit loyalty. Don't say that you can't wait to get to graduate school to better yourself or you hope to be in your own business in five years. Formulate answers that show you want to be in a better position *at their company* and that you're willing to accommodate their needs—rather than yours—first.

Crystal-Ball Gazing

More and more employers are using "situational questions" in hopes of better predicting employee behavior on the job. These can go something like this:

28. In your internships and part-time positions, what types of supervisors got the most out of you? Why?

29. What college professors did you most enjoy? Why?

30. What most influenced you to choose the career you're ready to begin?

31. When you're faced with a particularly tough decision, how do you go about making it? Can you give me an example from your college days?

32. The successful candidate for this position will be working with some highly trained indivi-

duals who have been with us for a long time. If
you get the job, how will you make sure that you
fit in?

33. What are you looking for in a job?

34. Let's say your supervisor gave you an assign-
    ment that you didn't understand and then left
    town for a week. Assume he or she is unreach-
    able.What would you do?

35. Have your hobbies or sports activities taught you
    any lessons that you'd bring to the job?

36. Describe your ideal boss.

37. This is a large (or a small) company. Do you
    think you'd like that sort of environment? Why?
    What do you think you might not like about it?

38. What do you know about the financial aspects of
    this business? Have any of your studies or read-
    ings helped you know about how we budget,
    what affects our bottom line?

39. Are you an organized person?

40. Do you manage your time well?

41. If your supervisor told you to do something a
    certain way, and you knew that way was dead
    wrong, what would you do?

42. You won't be managing people for a while. But
    if you were, how would your subordinates des-
    cribe you?

43. After you're on the job for a while, how will your
    co-workers describe you?

44. Why are you interested in this position?

45. How long do you think this position will be chal-
    lenging to you? What do you think you would
    like to do next?

46. Why this company? What about it appeals to you most?

47. Is there anything about this company or job that makes you apprehensive? Why?

48. What aspects of this job do you think you'll find the most interesting?

49. What aspects do you think you'll find least interesting?

50. How will you react to doing the least interesting or least pleasant parts of this job?

51. How do you think this job will help you achieve your long-term career objectives?

52. Describe your ideal job based on what you know of your discipline and this industry right now.

53. How do you think the job you're applying for matches up with that description?

54. Are there any glaring shortcomings to the position based on your description of the ideal job?

55. Were there any unusual difficulties you had to overcome to do so well in college? How did you do it?

56. What did you spend most of your time doing during your internship(s)?

57. Are you able to work overtime? On weekends?

58. Your lack of experience bothers me. Why do *you* think I should I hire someone just out of school, like you?

59. What do you want most out of your job—money? satisfaction? power?

60. Can you perform well under pressure? How do you know that?

What They're Trying This Time

All of these questions are designed to determine whether you have "organizational fit." The interviewer wants to know if you'll stick around for a while to become a valued employee, or whether the organization and/or you will soon wish you'd never heard of each other.

If you're a recent college graduate, you'll be at a distinct disadvantage in answering many of these questions. So:

- Admit when you don't have all of the answers. Or begin a lot of your answers with "I think..." or "From what I know about the company..."

- Remember the attributes the company wants most in its employees and display them every chance you get.

- Don't sound squeamish about going through the school of hard knocks. As mentioned in Chapter 7, many baby boomers think that baby busters (you) have a severe "attitude problem." Tell the interviewer, "Sure, I know this position has its share of unpleasant duties, but I'm sure everyone that's had this position has learned a lot by doing them."

- Be positive about your negatives.

- Don't be afraid to tell the interviewer that you'll ask for help in certain situations. Not many companies are looking for 22-year-old know-it-alls.

- Go in prepared with this winning answer about your ideal supervisor: "The ideal supervisor has a great deal of experience in the field and enjoys sharing it. I think he or she should delegate the challenging tasks of the department to the most deserving employees.

"(Management expert) Peter Drucker has said that 'the manager's role is to give employees the tools they need to get the job done.' I think that's a good description of the ideal supervisor—someone who provides the resources and, when necessary, the knowledge employees need to do and enjoy their jobs."

- If you don't really know where you want to be five or ten years down the road (and how many of us really do?), say so, but in a positive way. Your answer should be something like:

  "Well, I loved studying biochemistry and that's why I want to work at a leading company in the field, like yours. I hope that I can learn a great deal more about the field, and that I excel enough to be given additional challenges here. I'm only sure right now that I want to work and do well in this discipline."

- Dazzle 'em with footwork. Show off the research you've done on the company. Embellish your answers to these questions with facts you've learned about the company and the industry.

Wrapping Up

Just when you thought the grilling was over, the interviewer could very well have a crop of seemingly innocuous questions. Take them seriously. The interview ain't over till it's over.

61. Have you been interviewing for other positions?

62. Have you received any offers?

63. When do you have to hear from us? What is your availability?

64. What do you think of our compensation package?

65. How does this position seem to compare to others for which you've interviewed?

If you are interested in the position, don't be cute. Say that you are available immediately, or as soon as you can relocate—whatever is convenient for you and the employer. And tell the truth about other positions. You needn't bring up the names of the employers. Make it clear that the position for which you are interviewing is the one you're most interested in.

I also would advise against talking about salary at this stage. Get a sense of what the package (compensation and benefits) is, but wait until you get an offer to negotiate. That is the time when you have the most leverage.

---

66. Do You Have Any Questions?

This is the surefire sign that the interview is drawing to a close, and if you haven't asked a question until now, it's also probably a surefire bet that you're not getting the job.

You should be asking plenty of questions throughout the interview. If, at this point, you have all the information you need to make an informed decision, be decisive and say so.

If reading this list makes you feel as if you've run the gauntlet, remember you'll feel much worse after your interview if you fail to prepare to answer such most-asked questions.

Chapter 9

Are You Buying?

The Interview Is A Two-Way Street

I've continually emphasized that your main task during the interview is to sell yourself to the hiring manager and the company.

But if I left it at that, I'd be telling only half the story. During your interviews, you must also determine whether *you* are sold on the employer and the person who would become your immediate supervisor.

The interviews you'll experience with your prospective employer are your last and best chance to determine if *you* really want to work for the company and the hiring manager.

Of course, you can't do that very well if you approach the interview the way most candidates do—as if they are being interrogated by the police.

No, you must think of the interview as a conversation between two adults, both of whom are doing their best to impress each other.

Be determined that during your visits with the prospective employer, you will find out whether the job, the company, and the manager are right for **you**.

What You Want To
Know About The Job

Here are some questions you should ask of the screening interviewer and/or the hiring manager to make sure that the job you're applying for is right for you:

Can you give me a written description of the position, the major activities it involves, and the results expected?

If one does not exist, ask the interviewer to dictate as complete a description of the job to you as possible. Write down what he says. It might lead to other questions. It's a good idea to ask the screening interviewer for the job description so that you're prepared for your interview with the hiring manager with a series of penetrating, informed questions about exactly what the job requires.

Does this job usually lead to other positions at the company? Which ones?

Do you want to work at a dead-end job? Of course not. Find out where you can expect the position you're interviewing for to take you. Ask the interviewer what has happened to the person you would be replacing. Where did he or she go in the company? Is it realistic for you to hope for similar advancement?

Of course, while pursuing this line of questioning, you don't want to make it seem as if you can't wait to get out of a job you don't even have yet! Ask the questions in a completely non-threatening manner, expressing a modicum, but not an overabundance, of ambition.

Do people from this function and department usually get promoted to higher positions at the company?

Again, I remind you that you are part of the "twenty-something" generation that baby boomers are beginning to read, write, and complain about so much. Be careful that you don't appear *too* impatient to get a window office before it's perceived you have paid the appropriate dues.

Nevertheless, you want to have this information to make an informed decision. You don't want to wind up in one of the company's personnel backwaters.

Would you tell a qualified member of your family that he or she should pursue this job?

You're probably thinking: "I can't ask a question like that. The interviewer will think I'm off the wall."

Admittedly, the question is a little risky, but if you introduce it this way, "I have what might seem like a rather unusual question...", you'll appear self-confident, not cocky.

If the interviewer gives you a simple "yes", give him a simple "why?" You'll hear all of the good things he has to say about the position, and maybe some caveats as well.

Can You Really Work For This Boss?

You won't really get to know that much about the hiring manager unless you make an effort to peer behind the mask he's strapped on for the interview. A boss can make or break your success and enjoyment of a position. Here are some questions that will help you make an intelligent choice:

Can you tell me some of the particular skills or attributes that you want in the candidate for this position?

This can be your knockout punch. Not only will it tell you how much your boss will value the things you like most about yourself, but will help you know how you should shade the remainder of the interview.

For instance, if he says that he likes people that can work on their own, tell him about independent course work you've done.

If he says that he wants people who don't mind putting in 100 hours a week, make up your mind you'll look for another job.

During the past two years, how many people in your department been promoted? Were they promoted within the department or move on to other areas of the company?

A reasonable number will tell you that this boss is a good coach that doesn't hold his people down. If the people have moved to other departments at the company, it also indicates that he gives credit to his subordinates for the work of his department, rather than trying to steal all of the credit for himself.

If his turnover ratio has reached or exceeded Ted Williams' record batting average (.400 or 40%), you may be interviewing with a wolf in sheep's clothing. Put a hood over your head and run away.

Can you tell me a little bit about the people with whom I'll be working most closely?

I wish people had told me about this question before my last job interview! It can tell you many things—How good the people you are working with will be; how much you can learn from them; and, more importantly, whether the hiring manager is enthusiastic about his or her subordinates.

Remember, a hiring manager usually tries to put his best face on during an interview, just as the candidate does. He most likely will be in his most chipper mood. Asking about the people he supervises every day can let you get a glimpse behind the "game face."

If asking about his subordinates elicits no obvious enthusiasm, you probably won't enjoy working for that hiring manager. He probably attributes little of his success, but most of his headaches, to the people who work for him.

What do you like best about this company? Why?

This might seem like another one of those questions you *shouldn't* ask, but it's too good *not* to ask.

If the boss hems and haws a lot over this one, it indicates that he doesn't like the company that much at all.

If he's enthusiastic, his answer should help sell you on him and the company.

This question can give you a good sense of the values of the organization and the hiring manager. If he talks about nothing but products and how well his stock is doing, it indicates a lack of enthusiasm for the people side of the business.

What sort of performance appraisal system do you have at this company? How often do you review an employee's progress and set goals?

If the answer comes back any differently than "at least X times a year" (with "X" being *at least* one), start thinking about the next job you'll apply for. The absence of a performance planning and appraisal system indicates an absence of good management and low regard for employees.

No employee can develop without feedback.

Don't settle for a company not committed to developing its talent.

Will You Be Happy Working For This Company?

You might have the best boss and the best job in the world. But what good will that do if your boss resigns or you get transferred and the company is otherwise awful?

During your interview, the company should be selling you on the fact that it's a great place to work. Here are some questions to ask that will help fill in the blanks of your research into the organization:

What is the company's ranking within the industry? Does this position represent a change from where it was a few years ago?

You should have an answer to this question from your research, particularly if the company is publicly owned. If you have some of this information, build it into your question: "I've read that the company has risen from fifth to second in market share in just the last three years. What are the principle reasons for this dramatic move?"

Ideally, you'll hear explanations like "quality products," "concern for the customer," "great employees," rather than "smart financing" or "aggressive pricing." The more people-oriented the responses to your questions, the more appealing the company.

What are the organization's key strengths and weaknesses?

They'll probably ask you a similar question. Why not try it on them? Again, the answer will not only help you learn about the company, it will also tell you a great deal about your supervisor.

What do you like about this organization that you didn't find at other companies you've worked for?

This question takes some guts to ask, but most supervisors worth working for will admire your forthrightness. You're not putting your potential boss on the spot. You're trying to find out whether this company is right for you.

You might couch this question with an introduction like: "I don't have much exposure to the industry, of course, but you certainly do..."

Have you taken an employee opinion poll recently? Have any of the results been published?

This is another good question to ask the screening interviewer. Getting the information before your interview will help you ask some pointed questions.

Other questions you might want to consider to demonstrate your interest:

- *What new products is the company considering introducing over the next year or two?*
- *Has the organization had any layoffs or reductions in its work force over the past couple of years? Are any others anticipated? Was this department affected? How much (or little)?*
- *Is the company considering entering any new markets during the next few years? Which ones?*
- *You say you are anticipating a growth rate of X% over the next few years. Will this be achieved internally or through acquisitions?*

A Golden Opportunity

The interview is a golden opportunity to learn a great deal about the company, the boss, and the job you're trying to get.

Don't blow it by being too shy to ask these questions.

Asking for this information will make you feel more in control, will impress your interviewers, and will help you make one of the most important decisions of your life based on substantial data and intelligent analysis.

Chapter 10

What Did You Say?

Your Rights As An Interviewee

In an ideal world, companies and managers would judge their employees only on the basis of their job performance, and candidates would be judged only against a set of criteria deemed important for doing the job right.

Our world isn't ideal. And in the *real* world, many managers and entire companies discriminate, and few people can judge others with pure objectivity.

The most unpleasant manifestations of the real world for too many job candidates are questions and remarks related to sex, race, ethnic background, marital status, and all of the other ridiculous traits upon which the ignorant and sometimes not so ignorant think it fair to judge people.

What can you do if you come face to face with racism, sexism, or some other ugly "ism" during a job interview?

All too many candidates feel that they have to endure and answer politely every question an interviewer asks, no matter how distasteful or irrelevant.

That's pure nonsense. Candidates have rights. And the interviewer should know what these rights are. At the very least, *you* should know what your rights are.

This chapter will explain your rights as an interviewee and what you can do if you feel an interviewer has acted inappropriately or unlawfully.

What Does *That* Have To Do With My Job?

It's pretty easy to tell when a question is inappropriate —it has little or nothing to do with how the candidate might perform on the job. And that's pretty much what the law states—interviewers can ask questions that have to do with *job performance*. When they ask questions that are unrelated to the work to be performed, they could be walking on thin ice.

Every state has fair-employment-practices laws governing the screening of job candidates and lists of questions considered unlawful for employers to ask on job applications and during interviews. Check with your state's Fair Employment Practices Commission for more details.

In the meantime, I can give you the following general guidelines that may help you recognize discriminatory or otherwise illegal interview and job application questions:

- *Name*. Sure, that seems innocent enough. Employers will need your name to give you a paycheck, if for no other reason. But in many states you are protected from questions that seek to determine your birth name if you've had it legally changed, or, if you are a married woman, your maiden name. However, employers *are* permitted to ask what other names they should check to determine your employment history.

- *Creed*. Under no circumstances is an employer permitted to ask about your religious affiliation or the religious holidays you observe. In addition, interviewers are not permitted to make even simple statements such as, "This is a Christian (or Jewish, or Muslim) company." Perhaps they are looking for some sort of reaction from the prospective employee, and plan to make a hiring decision based on that "pro" or "con" reaction.

- *Nationality.* Employers are generally forbidden to ask about your ancestry, descent, parentage, or nationality, that of your parents or spouse, or inquire about your "mother tongue." Technically speaking, an interviewer could not ask, "Is that an Irish name?" but he *could* ask you what language(s) you are proficient in.

- *Race.* Employers cannot ask you about the color of your skin or that of your relatives or spouse.

- *Sex.* Employers are not permitted to ask about a candidate's marital status or plans for marriage. Likewise, they are forbidden from asking women about their plans for having children.

- *Military service.* The employer can ask how long and in what branch of the service you were in, but not the type of discharge you received.

- *Age.* Employers cannot ask for your birth date or about facts that might reveal your birth date, such as the year you graduated from high school.

- *Physical condition.* Employers can ask if you have any physical conditions that might impede your performance on the job, but they cannot ask something like, "Do you have any physical disabilities?"

- *Photograph.* Employers are not allowed to ask you to affix a photograph to your job application.

- *Organizations.* Employers can ask about the applicant's membership in organizations that *the applicant* considers important to the performance of the job.

How To React When Asked
The Wrong Question

Despite a plethora of lawsuits charging employers with discriminatory hiring practices over the past 25 years, unlawful questions still are commonly asked during interviews. This is particularly true of interviews by hiring managers, who generally have not received the extensive education on legal issues personnel professionals now routinely undergo.

What do you do if you're asked an unlawful question you believe you shouldn't have to answer?

You have three choices:

1. You can be a Constitutionalist and refuse on principle to answer any unlawful question, even if you'd come up smelling like a rose.

2. You can be a pragmatist and provide any answers you feel wouldn't hurt you, while you tactfully sidestep illegal questions you think *could* hurt you.

3. You can use a mixture of both approaches.

Let's say you have an "obviously" Italian last name, like Rutigliano. You greet the interviewer and he says, "Boy, that's Italian, isn't it?" You should smile politely and not answer at all. It's quite possible he meant absolutely no offense.

However, if later the interviewer pursues the line of questioning with, "Were your parents born in the United States or on the other side?", you can dodge it one more time by saying something like, "They don't remember. They were just little babies." But by now you should be wary for any further signs of prejudice or insensitivity.

If the interviewer still doesn't get the hint, and continues to allude to your Italian heritage, then you should point out to him that he is doing something illegal. You might say, "I really don't see what my ancestry has to do with my application for this job. You must know that your not supposed to ask me questions like this."

Believe it or not, you could still stay on the interviewer's good side if you handle the situation in a diplomatic way. At the same time, you will have put him on notice that you are aware of the law and do not take it as lightly as he obviously does. You also have told him that he has opened himself up to a discrimination charge.

Such a line of questioning, however, might well indicate that you don't want to work for this supervisor under any circumstances. He's obviously an ignorant, insensitive person. Take the job only if you are desperate.

They Are Usually Much More Subtle

However, many employers or supervisors that discriminate will try to elicit information they consider damaging in more subtle ways.

For instance, an interviewer might ask older applicants what year they graduated college. Or ask someone he suspects of being an immigrant if English is spoken at home.

Here's a case of a *really* subtle form of discrimination. A friend of mine applied for a job at one of the big tobacco concerns. She went through three interviews, and the company was obviously very high on her. During her last interview, she was asked if she would like a cigarette. She said, "No thanks. I don't smoke," and that was the last she heard from them.

Notice, the interviewer never asked, "Are you a smoker?" or "Do you smoke?" Turning down an applicant because she refused to engage in an unhealthy activity might put the company on questionable legal and public relations ground.

But the information was gotten nevertheless, and the hiring decision was made based on that illicit information.

(When I heard the story, I couldn't help but wish she had answered, "No thanks. I don't smoke *during inter-views.*" Perfectly true, and nearly as coy as their gambit!)

Still another female acquaintance, Karen, interviewed at one of the largest companies in the U.S. The skilled interviewer kept shifting gears between very job-related and very personal questions.

Though Karen was a savvy interviewee and had little trouble deflecting the questions she knew to be inappropriate, she let her guard down once, beginning an answer with "My husband..."

The interviewer pounced as quickly as a salesman's foot in an open door. She began asking questions about what the husband did and how he "felt about his wife having a job."

The interviewer apparently wanted to know what Karen's career and family plans were, but knew better than to come right out and ask such unlawful questions.

Once *Karen* introduced the subject of her husband, however, the interviewer felt her "family life" was fair game. After all, she didn't want to ask anything as obviously unlawful as, "Are you married?" or "Don't you want to have children, and won't your career interfere with that."

She just wanted to know the *answers* to those questions.

Therefore, I'd advise you never to bring up personal material that you might not want to talk about in more detail. Savvy interviewers will grab at the opportunity to get information they want without running the risk of ending up in court. Their defense will be, "*I* never asked about her family; *she* brought it up."

And while it still might not be entirely "up and up," it may well prove enough of a defense.

What To Do After The Fact

If you are not offered a position after being asked unlawful questions, you *might* have grounds for charging the employer with discrimination. The interviewer asked non-job-related questions, and you have reason to believe that your refusal to answer these questions or the answers you provided led to your not being hired.

The operative word here is "might." You would have to prove that the questions were asked for the purpose of discriminating among applicants for an illegal reason.

For instance, if the manager asking all those questions about Italian ancestry subsequently hired another Italian, you wouldn't have much of a claim despite the fact that you *were* asked illegal questions.

If you *do* think that you have grounds for a charge of discrimination, you should file your charges simultaneously with the appropriate state agency and the federal government's Equal Employment Opportunity Commission (EEOC). The EEOC generally will wait until the state agency has conducted an investigation, then conduct an investigation of its own.

As you would expect when dealing with government agencies, you might not hear anything for years, and when they do act, it is solely to determine whether there is reason to believe your charge is true. Therefore, if you are anxious for justice, you should request that the EEOC issue you a notice to sue 180 days after you file your charge.

If You Are Right

If the EEOC determines in you favor, it will attempt to mediate the dispute between you and the employer. Failing to arrange for such an agreement, the Commission will either file a suit or issue you a letter giving you the right to sue the employer. You must file your suit within 90 days of receiving such a letter.

Even if you go through all this trouble and win your lawsuit, don't expect to receive one of those colossal jury awards that seem to occur weekly on "L.A. Law." The most you'll probably get from the employer is about one year's salary.

As I've stressed throughout this book, the primary thing to remember about interviews is that you are there as a participant, not as a helpless victim.

If you feel that the interviewer is asking you questions that shouldn't be asked, the first step is to try to shrug them off and change the direction of the conversation.

The next step is to inform the employer that you know he or she is doing something unlawful. This will give him or her a subtle warning that you won't submit to illegal interview behavior, or the discrimination that might result from it, without a fight.

The last step is to terminate the interview and, possibly, seek to bring formal charges against the company and the interviewer.

Important note: None of the advice in this chapter should be construed as constituting legal advice. I am not an attorney. If you feel a would-be employer has discriminated against you, you should contact the appropriate government agencies and a competent attorney to assess your rights and options under state and federal law.

Chapter 11

Bet You're Glad That's Over

But It's Not—Until You Follow Up

Yogi Berra said many memorable things, most of them head-scratchers, but none as famous as the line, "It ain't over 'til it's over." If the interview is to prove meaningful for you, and you want to increase your chances of landing that job—even if you're utterly sure that you knocked the interviewer's socks off—the interview ain't over when you leave your would-be employer's office.

No, to increase your chances of landing that job, you must take several follow-up steps.

Don't Be Just Another Candidate

I hope you'll learn at least one great lesson from every boss you'll have during your career. One of my most memorable bosses taught me several lessons that I find myself applying at least once every week.

The single most valuable lesson he taught me was that the world was full of mediocre people. It is, therefore, relatively easy (he asserted) to be perceived as excellent, so easy that it makes no sense *not* to take steps to rise above the crowd. The first thing to remember is to act promptly. When you meet someone who might be important to you, write a letter and see that it's mailed that very day. Think how great you'll look next to the hundreds of people who have said that they'd contact that person and never did, or did so...weeks later.

Take my word for it, that's great advice.

On the day of your interview, use it. Do not pass Go. Proceed directly to your word processor, type a letter to the person who interviewed you, and walk it to the post box.

The letter should express gratitude for the chance to be considered for the position. It should, like the initial cover letter you sent, emphasize one of your key strengths. It should include some mention of something you or the interviewer said.

Most importantly, the follow-up letter should let the "real you" show through. After all, you are now writing to someone you've met and who, presumably, has gotten to know you pretty well.

There's a good example of dynamite follow-up letter on page 133.

Giving References

If the interviewer asks for a list of references, tell him you will get back to him with a list that afternoon or, if it already *is* afternoon, the next day.

Does this make you seem unprepared? Shouldn't you go into the interview with the list already prepared? After all, your resume says, "References available upon request," and here's the request.

Well, in the world of interviews, stalling for a little time before giving the references is SOP [standard operating procedure].

Robert N. Johnsmeyer

725 The Crescent, Manhattan Beach, CA 90000-0001
213/777-3434

September 4, 1991

Mr. John Edelstein
Vice President/Distribution
ABD Neckwear
11200 Stemmons
Boston, MA 02222

Dear Mr. Edelstein:

It certainly was a pleasure meeting with you today and learning more about the entry-level dispatching position at ABD Neckwear. Thank you once again for your time and for the information you shared with me.

I feel confident that my education in cartography will be invaluable in helping the company achieve the most efficient use of its fleet. Your department's achievements in distribution are extraordinary, and I'm sure I would find the environment stimulating and challenging. I was especially interested in your description of the employee suggestion system that has helped the company realize important savings.

Mr. Edelstein, I found our time together today not only informative, but enjoyable. I am sure that we would greatly enjoy working together.

I look forward to hearing from you in the very near future.

Sincerely yours,

Robert N. Johnsmeyer

The reason you want to wait is that you'll want to tell your prospective references that a call might be coming from Mr. Somebody of ABC Corporation. If they are going to give you a good reference, they should be prepared. And if they're not, you'll want to change the list...fast.

How Do You Know What They'll Say?

You've worked too hard to get this job to let a reference check blow it for you. You should manage that process as well as you've managed every other part of the interview.

The first step is to line up your references before going on your first interview. You should speak to all of the people you'll be putting on your list and let them know how you will be presenting yourself and what exactly you'll be saying about your affiliation with them.

It's a good idea to follow these conversations up with a letter and a copy of your resume. This will allow the reference to see just how the job or internship or independent course work is presented and will tell him what you are saying about your abilities and accomplishments.

Unsure about what one of these references might say about you? Ask him. If you feel that he or she remembers your relationship differently, correct him.

Still unsure? Then, do a little detective work. Have a friend of yours call and say that he is in the personnel department of ABC company and that you've applied for a job there. This will allow you to learn exactly what the person will say about you.

More Sounds Of Silence

In these litigious times, many references are afraid to say anything about a past associate for fear of being sued for libel or slander. Therefore, you should be aware of the things that your references *won't* say.

If you know that a reference will give only the bare facts of date of employment and job title, try your best to leave him or her off the list. Employers might read unwillingness to say *any*thing as merely avoidance of saying anything *bad*.

Softening The Blow

But no matter how careful you are at this stage of the process, there's a chance that the manager or professor with an unfavorable opinion of you will be contacted. If you think this might damage your chances of securing the job you covet, do your best to score a preemptive strike. Tell the hiring manager or personnel department why you might receive an unfavorable reference from that manager. One of the most common and easily accepted reasons for a bad reference is the vague "personality conflict."

Indicate that you and the manager did not get along, but that there are other people at the organization who can vouch for the quality of your work. Give one of their names.

Follow Up

It's a good idea to follow up with your references to see if they were called and, if they were, how the questioning went. What were some of the things that your prospective employer wanted to know? Is it obvious from their questions that one particular area of your background is troubling them?

If that's the case, you might be able to overcome their objections with a follow-up phone call a week to ten days after the interview.

It's perfectly acceptable for you to inquire about the status of the position. Have they filled it? Do they expect to reach a decision in the near future? When? Are you still in the running?

This phone call will give the interviewer an opportunity to ask you about anything he's heard during the reference check that makes him feel uncomfortable.

Changed Your Mind?

Did something during the interview make you decide that you didn't want to work at the company?

Then politely take yourself out of the running. Write a letter to the screening interviewer and the hiring manager indicating that you thank them for the opportunity to interview, but have decided to pursue other options.

You never know: Someday you might decide that company is perfect for you. Following up on the interview professionally will ensure that your file in the personnel department has *good* things to say about you, not comments like "unreliable," "indecisive," "schlemiel" or worse.

No Job Is Over Until The Paperwork Is Done

Remember: Write a thank-you letter on the day of your interview, follow up with your references, and respond promptly to all of the interviewers' requests for more information.

Your prompt attention to these matters is an almost sure way to stand out from the crowd of candidates.

And just one more indication of what a terrific, prompt employee you will be.

Chapter 12

Back In The Classroom Again

Did You Learn Anything From The Interview?

What did you learn from your interview? Did you use it as an opportunity to soak up as much information as you could about your prospective employer? Or, were you so white with fright that you barely remembered to breathe?

As I've stressed time and again, the interview is a two-way street. It is an opportunity for the employer to learn about you and vice versa. You should learn as much as you can about the employer, not only by asking some of the questions discussed in Chapter 9, but by observing the offices, the attitudes of interviewers and other people you come into contact with, and any nuances in the way your interviews were conducted.

Seemed Like A Good
Idea At The Time

My friend Tony is a crackerjack writer and editor. His work brought him into fairly frequent contact with Bill, a public relations "flack" for a large consulting firm.

Tony was struggling and not making much money, so
his antennae went up when Bill moved on to another consulting outfit as head of public relations. Bill's job would be
to build a complete public relations staff and program from
scratch. Tony, having heard all about Bill's house in an
expensive suburb, his family's annual trips to Europe, and
the new Mercedes, wanted to know just when Bill would be
hiring staff at QRS Consulting.

Tony didn't have to wait too long. Bill not only told him

he was a "shoe-in" for the lucrative job. However, he would
have to meet with the director of human resources and the
vice president of communications before he was officially
hired.

Bill seemed very happy in his new job, so Tony was
initially excited about the interviews

When they were over, Tony decided he wouldn't take the
job if it paid twice as much.

What happened during the interviews?

Well, Tony picked up so many "negative vibes" during
his screening that he knew he would absolutely loathe
QRS. For instance, in his interview with Mr. Ego, the
director of human resources, he was asked almost no questions. Ego talked about what an exciting place QRS was
and how hard everyone worked. His favorite phrases were
"kicking butt and taking down names" and "show 'em no
mercy", he used "I" and "me" an insufferable number of
times, and he seemingly couldn't have cared less when
Tony tried to say something about himself.

The vice president of communications was even worse.
He talked on and on about how hard everyone at QRS
worked, how many nights *he* had to work "all kinds of
hours," how arbitrary the many last-minute changes made
by the company president often were.

At the end of the ordeal, Bill took Tony for a bite in the
company cafeteria. Tony saw a lot of people practically running down the food line, wolfing down their sandwiches

while they read work-related materials, then rushing back to their offices. It was the quietest cafeteria he'd ever seen —nobody had time to eat.

Tony's spirits were somewhere below the linoleum, but Bill was still giving the company, his department, and his job high marks. He loved it.

Ego called Tony to offer him the job next day. Tony said he'd have to think it over and Ego acted as if Tony had rocks in his head. "What could there be to think about?" Ego blustered. "We're offering you a lot of money, and we'll be as big as IBM some day."

Tony called Bill the next day to say that he wouldn't be joining QRS. Bill was dumbfounded when Tony gave his reasons: "Neither Ego nor your boss asked me a simple question about me or my qualifications. All they did was talk about how hard they worked. QRS is strictly for Type A personalities, and it couldn't care less about its employees as long as they stay late."

Bill put up a mild argument and told Tony that he had gotten the wrong impression. Tony told Bill not to expect him to change his mind this sunspot cycle.

Bill, citing the hours and the poor way his department was treated, quit QRS less than six months later.

Take Stock

This is only a slight exaggeration of a true story and it demonstrates that your job during the interview is not only to impress the company, but to become a sponge soaking up impressions. Is this going to be a good place to work? Is your boss going to be friend or foe? Are your colleagues going to work with you and support you or quietly trace targets on your back?

After you get home from the interview, write and mail your thank-you letters, and contact those you've given as references, sit down in a quiet room with a pen and paper and write down all of your impressions about the company and the people you met. Don't worry about being grammatically correct or especially descriptive. Just record all of your impressions, good and bad. Here are some questions that might help:

• What were your impressions of the people you came into contact with *other* than the interviewers? Did they seem happy to be at work, or did the place feel like a funeral parlor...at midnight? Were people open, friendly, cordial and relaxed, or uptight, rushed and brusque? (If you could practically see people's nerve endings, you probably should look for a job somewhere else.)

• Did the interviewers seem genuinely interested in you or only in your qualifications? Were you treated like an individual or a commodity?

• Did your boss seem like a workaholic? Was his desk teeming with papers? Did he talk about long hours and all of the details he had to oversee? Did he mention other staff at all?

    Avoid working for the work-obsessed. You can never do enough for them; they will never give you a lot of responsibility; and they probably will be stingy with compliments and credit for your accomplishments. Workaholics are insecure people convinced no one can do the job as well as they can. No matter how terrific you are, you won't convince a workaholic boss to give you the running room you need or want.

• What does your instinct tell you? There's something to be said for "going with your gut." Do you think you'd get along with the boss? Would he be overly critical or helpful and supportive?

• How did the interviewers react to your questions? Did they seem to welcome the opportunity to give you information, or were they reticent to share, annoyed with you for putting them to the test? If the latter, think long and hard about how they'll act *after* you take the job—they'll probably display even less patience and willingness to share.

- What did your boss's eyes tell you? Did he engage in a staring contest, study you for clues to your emotions, overly enjoy the role of the Grand Inquisitor? Or was he friendly, open, honest and caring?

Keep Your Eyes Peeled

Usually a company will convey a great deal about itself on bulletin boards, on the walls and display cases of reception areas, in its main corridors. Are there employee awards posted, or does the company give no recognition of its employees' accomplishments? Are there aphorisms posted here and there? Do they say something like, "If YOU aren't proud of it, don't ship it"? Or are they more like something you'd see in a government institution: "Radio-playing is grounds for termination"?

Look for all of the telltale clues that you can. Think about them and write down your impressions. If you are offered a job with the company, you will be faced with one of the biggest decisions of your life. Make sure you're appropriately armed with all of the information you need to make the right one.

Chapter 13

Negotiating Your First Salary

You Want To Be *Paid* For Working Here?

There are many schools of thought on the question of salary discussions during job interviews. Some experts advise bringing the topic to a head as soon as possible after the preliminary part of the interview. Others advise avoiding the subject entirely, as if getting a paycheck were some unspeakable practice.

Common sense dictates a course somewhere between these two extremes. I recommend that you avoid bringing up the subject of salary yourself during your screening and selection interviews. If the interviewer brings it up, answer his or her questions. But it's really in your best interest to avoid getting down to the brass tacks of salary negotiation until the offer stage, which I'll discuss later.

A Buy-Sell Situation

The interview is a classic buy-sell situation. You are trying to sell yourself to a company and get the best price you can. The company is making sure that it wants to buy what you're offering, and, naturally, hopes to pay as little as you'll accept.

Not talking about price in a situation like this is ludicrous. But talking about it at the wrong time is foolish.

This brings to mind the example of Barry, whose story we read in Chapter 7. When he was told about the position he eventually secured, the executive recruiter told him that the job was paying a top salary of $40,000. Barry was seeking $50,000.

Barry—who, of course, was much more experienced at job hunting than you are right now—firmly told the recruiter, "I want that job. Send me on the interview. After they've met me, they'll be willing to pay me what I want."

It sounded cocky, but Barry was absolutely right. He studiously avoided the subject of salary during the entire interview. When the interviewer finally asked, "What would it take to get you over here?", Barry said, "I understand the job has a top salary of $40,000." He waited for the interviewer to nod, then said, "Well, I would need more than that. I came here because the job sounded terrific. In fact, the job description Helen (the recruiter) gave me had my name written all over it."

Eventually the employer came around to meet his demand. But only because Barry had already *sold* himself.

Timing Is Everything In Life

This example should point out the biggest truism about salary discussion: *You have nothing to gain by discussing dollars and cents before you've convinced the employer that you're the right person for the job.*

Most probably you won't find yourself in a situation similar to Barry's. Just getting out of college, you'll be applying for entry-level positions that have relatively narrow salary ranges. What's more, you don't really have that much to sell yet.

Nevertheless, you are not a commodity. If you can stand apart from the crowd of applicants, if you can convince the employer that an extra couple of thousand dollars would be well spent on a dynamo like you, then one of the only sure ways *not* to get it is by putting a price tag around your neck too early in the proceedings.

Along with time off, salary and benefits is one subject that you should not bring up yourself. After all, the interview is the company's chance to get to know you. How can the interviewer know what he or she is willing to pay you until the learning process is over?

In Chapter 7, I stressed that showing an interest in the interviewer is critically important. Trying to speak about something—salary—that he has no *desire* to speak about until he finishes his questions is one sure way to make the interviewer feel that you are self-absorbed and uninterested in him and his questions.

Would you buy something from a salesperson who only wanted to impress upon you how much something cost?

Of course not.

Why would a company hire someone only interested in seeing how much he or she could get?

I, and most experienced hiring managers I know, have at least one story about candidates who ask *only* about salary, benefits, and days off during the entire interview. None of these subjects is a good one to ask about when the employer first asks you if you have any questions!

What If The Interviewer Brings It Up First?

You can always tell when an interviewer knows he's paying people too little—he'll bring up salary early to determine whether he can afford you before spending the time to interview you.

That might not *always* be the reason that the subject of salary is broached too early. It might just be the inexperience of the interviewer or his premonition that you'll want more than he can afford.

Whatever the reason, if it *does* come up too early, the subject of salary should be sidestepped. Remember: *It can't possibly do you any good to discuss salary before you've sold the employer.*

So, handle the question as you would some of the sensitive questions we discussed at the beginning of the last chapter—diplomatically avoid them. One of the following replies might prove useful:

- *"I have an idea of the salary range of the position from your ad (or from what the recruiter said). That sounds like a reasonable range to me."*

- *"I'm not quite sure what I want. I'd like to hear a little more about what my responsibilities will be."*

- *"I'm willing to consider any reasonable salary offer."*

- *"From what I know about the position and the company, I don't think we'll have any trouble agreeing on a fair salary."*

Remember, you DON'T want to talk about money even though the employer brought it up. Defer, defer, defer the discussion until later.

Fielding The Offer

So, you're an ace candidate. You impress the interviewer and a couple of days later you get an offer by phone.

You're delirious. You want to shout with joy. After all, you've sold a stranger on yourself. You've gotten a terrific vote of confidence. YOU GOT A JOB!

That's all completely understandable. But don't get carried away. You've just captured the high ground in your search for a job. Be sure to exploit it.

Earlier in the chapter, I again stressed that the interview is a buy-sell situation. Now that the company is sold on you, you're the one who must make the decision to buy.

Take your time. You should never—repeat, NEVER—accept a job the minute it's offered to you. Even though you've probably thought about little else since your last interview with the employer, and have thoroughly made up your mind that you will accept the job if it's offered, tell the company that you need some time to consider it.

You could say you want to sleep on it, or think about it over the weekend, or talk it over with your spouse or fiance or "advisor."

After you receive the offer, you must consider the *reality* of the offer—the fact that you will be working at the company for (hopefully!) quite some time.

Most companies will push you for a fairly quick response. The company has probably interviewed other promising candidates for the position and doesn't want to lose them if their leading candidate turns them down.

However, don't act before *you're* ready to. Tell the person making the offer that you need a short time to think it over, thank him or her profusely for thinking so highly of you, and agree on a day and a time that you'll call back with your answer.

If The Salary Isn't What You Had In Mind...

Most often, college graduates entering the job market will be interviewing for positions with a narrow salary range—$16,000 to $18,000, $24,000 to $27,000, etc., depending on the profession and industry.

If you are offered a salary close to the top of that range —$17,500 or $26,000 in the above examples—consider it a compliment and don't think too hard about pushing for more money. You don't have that much to gain anyway.

But if you're offered a salary at the floor of the range, push for some more money. Tell the interviewer, "I understood that the position was paying in the range of $21,000 to $24,000. Why are you offering me only $21,500? I know that I don't have any experience, but none was called for in the advertisement (or position description)."

This will usually encourage the interviewer to come up in his offer a bit, though he might have been saving the top end for people with more advanced degrees or some experience in the field (despite what the ad said).

If you're still leaning toward the position, ask when you will receive your first salary review. If the answer is on your anniversary date, see if you can at least push for an earlier review to make up some of the shortfall between the offer and your expectations.

Tell the person making the offer, "I am very flattered by the offer and I wish we could agree on a higher salary. How about if you give me my first salary review in, say, six months, rather than twelve?"

This is a rather easy concession for the interviewer to make. He will think that he is getting the candidate he wants for only half the difference between what you want to earn and what he wants to pay.

How Am I Supposed To Live On This?

This might be a case of closing the barn door after the cow has escaped.

But if you are very surprised at the low salary offers you are getting during your first interviews, then you're, to quote our President, in deep doo doo.

As you prepare to embark on a career, you should make sure that it is one that will fulfill your needs. And if high salary is one of them, you'd better be aiming for a profession or technical discipline. If you expect to get $50,000 a year (or $30,000, for that matter) in your first job in, say, publishing, you're in for a rude awakening.

Before you go on your first interview, you should have gained, through your research, a pretty good idea of the numbers employers will be discussing with you when the question of salary comes up. If you're shocked the first time salary comes up during an interview, you are in for a bumpy ride on your way to your first job.

Ask All Of Those Questions You Couldn't Ask Before

Once you're happy with the salary offer, it's time to ask about all of those matters we advised you *not* to ask about during your interviews. Get the details on the company's health benefits and vacation policy, life insurance, company cars, anything and everything that's part of your compensation package.

Most company vacation policies are fairly standard: two weeks for the first three years, three weeks thereafter. Benefits might call for varying amounts of employee contributions. A number of benefits—profit sharing, company car, etc.—may not be immediately available to you.

Generally speaking, neither benefits nor vacations should be major factors in your decision. You should have learned something about them much earlier than this; if they were so abysmal, why are you still considering the job offer?

If there *are* any other questions you feel will actually affect you decision of whether to accept the offer, you had better ask them now!

Okay, Yogi

After all this work, I'm assuming you finally accepted an offer...somewhere! And that they're even going to pay you.

Breathe a sigh of relief, and sit back to listen to Rosanne Barr sing the National Anthem.

It's over.

You got a job.

Congratulations!

Now get ready for the *real* work.

Index

Your First Interview

Activities data input sheet, 50-51
Awards & honors data input sheet, 52

Berra, Yogi, 131
Body language, 86-88
Bosses, work-obsessed, 140

Campus recruiters, 16-17
Career Directory Series, 12
College data input sheet, 49
College Placement Annual, 13
College Placement Directory, 12
Concentration, importance of, 95-96
Cost of hire, 56
Cover letter, 22
  appearance, 23
  contents, 23-24

Cover letter (cont.)
  follow-up, 28-32
  importance of, 24
  sample, 25, 27

Data input sheets, 37ff
Data input sheets, forms, 43-54
Database interview, 55, 63-64
Discrimination, 123
Dress, 84-86
  men, 84-85
  women, 85
Dun & Bradstreet directories, 13

Employee benefits, when to ask questions about, 149
Employee opinion polls, 120
Employment data input sheet, samples, 43-45
Employment records, 35, 37

Encyclopaedia of Associations, 13
Equal Employment Opportunity Commission, 129
Evaluating the job opportunity
  co-workers, 140
  how to, 139-141
  office environment, 141
  using your intuition, 140
  workaholic boss, 140
Extracurricular activities, 36

F&S Index of Corporations and Industries, 13
Fielding the offer, 146-147
Fitch Corporations Manuals, 13
Follow-up letter to interview, 132, 133 (sample)
Follow-up phone call, 28

Graduate school data input sheet, 49

Handshake, 86
High school data input sheet, 48
Hiring manager
  can you work for this person? 117
  coping with, 72-74
  disadvantages of interviewing with, 69-71
  importance of contacting, 22
  inspiring confidence in, 71-72
Honors and awards, 36

Illegal questions, 124-125
  about affiliations, 125
  about age, 125
  about military service, 125
  about name, 124
  about nationality, 125
  about physical condition, 125
  about race, 125
  about religion, 124-125
  how to respond to, 126-127
  what to do after the fact, 129
Illegal requirements, photographs, 125
Interview, interviewing
  and body language, 86-88
  and concentration, 95-96
  and importance of listening, 96
  and relaxing for, 88-90
  changing your mind about the job, 136
  database technique, 55
  demonstrating interest in interviewer, 90-94
  different techniques, 55
  dress for, 84-86
  exhibiting knowledge of company, 17-18, 19
  follow-up letter, 132
  handshake, 86
  positive action words to use, 94-95
  questions about the boss, 117-119
  questions about the company, 119-121
  questions about your co-workers, 118
  questions, open-ended, 98

Interview, interviewing (cont.)
  selective process, 8, 56
  silence as a technique, 98-99
  situational technique, 55
  small talk, 87
  stress technique, 55
  taking control of, 78-79
  talking about yourself, 74-78
"It ain't over 'til it's over," 131

Job description, 116

Language data input sheet, 54
Listening, 20, 95-96

MacRae's Bluebook, 13
Military records, 36
Military service data input
  sheet, 53
Moody's Manuals, 13

Performance appraisal systems, 119
Personal information
  education, 38
  employment records, 35, 37
  extracurricular activities,
    36, 38
  foreign languages, 39
  honors and awards, 36, 38
  importance of knowing, 42
  military records, 36, 38-39
  talking about yourself, 74-78
  volunteer activities, 35, 38
Personnel department, 22
  when to contact, 26

Post-interview, evaluating the
  job, 139-141
Pre-screen interview, phone
  call, 30
Preparing for the interview,
  33-54
Promotion opportunities, 116

Questions
  about your co-workers, 118
  asked by interviewee, 12,
    17, 20, 114
  asked by interviewee, 116
  asked of interviewee, 103
  coping with, 107-108, 112-113
  employee opinion polls, 120
  getting to know you, 106-107
  importance of asking, 121
  open-ended, 98
  performance appraisal sys-
    tems, 119
  promotion opportunities, 116
  situational technique, 109-111
  "Tell me about yourself,"
    74-75
  what you've accomplished,
    104-105
  wrap-up, 113-114

References, 132-135
  follow-up, 135
  notifying yours, 134
  why postpone giving them,
    134
Relaxing, tips, 88-90
Researching prospective
  companies
    annual reports, 15

Researching prospective
  companies (cont.)
    books, 14-15
    business editors, 14
    business/industry
      associations, 13-14
    campus recruiters, 16-17
    chambers of commerce,
      13
    college placement office,
      12
    employee handbooks, 15-
      16
    importance of, 11-12, 17-18
    placement agencies, 14
    sales/marketing bro-
      chures, 16
    school alumni, 14
    stock brokers/analysts,
      14
    through library, 12-13
    what you should learn, 21

Salary
  a buy-sell situation, 143-144
  entry-level ranges of, 144
  how to ask for more, 148
  when the interviewer
    brings it up too early, 145-
    146
  when to discuss, 143-146
Screening interview
  live, 60-67
  telephone, 57-60
Situational interview, 55, 65
  coping with, 66
Skilled interviewers,
  advantages of, 69
Small talk, 87

Standard & Poor's Register of
  Corporations, Directors and
  Executives, 13
Stress interview, 55, 62-63
  coping with, 63
Structured interview, see also
  Database interview
  coping with, 65

Targeted interview, 64-65
  coping with, 65
Thomas Register of American
  Companies, 13

Volunteer activities, 35, 38
Volunteer work data input
  sheet, 46-47

Words, positive action, 94-95